TRACING FAMILY HISTORY IN WALES:
how to read the inscriptions
on Welsh gravestones

TRACING FAMILY HISTORY IN WALES:
how to read the inscriptions on Welsh gravestones

Gwen Awbery

ISBN: 978-1-84524-168-1

Cover design: Eirian Evans

First edition: 2010
Llygad Gwalch, Ysgubor Plas, Llwyndyrys,

☎: 01758 750432   📠: 01758 750438

✉: llyfrau@carreg-gwalch.com
Website: www.carreg-gwalch.com

Contents

Preface

I was asked recently why I wanted to write this handbook, and indeed why I find gravestones so interesting. The answer goes right back to my childhood and my grandfather Edgar Jenkins, a monumental mason who had built a house and workshop up on the mountainside, next to the cemetery. I can remember watching him as he carved the lettering on the stones and filled in the gold leaf. When my sister and I got in the way, we would be sent off to play in the cemetery, and would wander around admiring the flowers on the graves and the carved angels. When I began later on to trace the history of the family, I found that he came, in fact, from a long line of stonemasons, reaching back at least to the beginning of the nineteenth century.

It is hardly surprising that, many years later, this fascination with gravestones and the inscriptions carved on them should resurface. I am by training a linguist, and my research has always focused on the Welsh language. Here was an unexplored wealth of information about the way ordinary people were using the language, and this over a long period of time. In which districts are there inscriptions in Welsh? Are they confined to a particular period? Do they vary from one area to another? I have spent many happy hours in Welsh churchyards, burial grounds and cemeteries, looking for the answers to questions of this kind.

And this is where the handbook comes in. I have often, while making notes in a churchyard, come across someone who was looking for a family grave but couldn't understand the Welsh wording on the stones. Could I help? Yes, of course. We would look around and find the right grave, and I would explain how to read the inscription. I gradually realised that this was a problem faced by many people who do not speak Welsh, but whose ancestors were at one time Welsh-speaking and are commemorated by Welsh inscriptions. This handbook is an attempt to fill the gap, and make accessible this amazing resource to everyone who is researching family history in Wales.

Acknowledgements

The photographs showing partial inscriptions, which appear at the end of each chapter in this book, were taken in the churchyards, chapel burial grounds and civic cemeteries listed below. I am grateful to the church, chapel and civic authorities, who in every case readily gave permission for their use.

Parish Churches: Brynhenllan; Llangynwyd; Moylegrove; Pentyrch; St Dogmael's.
Chapels: Bethel, Sketty, Swansea; Caersalem Newydd, Tirdeunaw, Swansea; Croesyparc, Peterston-super-Ely; Ramah, Dinas; Saron, Letterston; Seion, Glais, Swansea; Tabor, Dinas.
Civic Cemetery: Heath Cemetery, Cardiff.

I am also grateful to Rhiannon Weber, and to the chapel authorities of Nazareth Chapel, Llwynhendy, for permission to use the photograph which appears on the back of the cover.

I would like to thank Jen Llywelyn for her helpful comments and encouragement in the preparation of this book; and Paul Meara who has spent many hours over the years discussing the issues of principle which arise in working with inscriptions, and the practical problems which need to be solved to carry out this work.

Introduction

Tracing family history is a fascinating process. You trawl through census records, parish registers, old newspapers, maps and photographs, letters and diaries. You visit county archives, go on-line, rummage in the attic. All to fill in the gaps of what you know already, and find out who your family were, what they did for a living, where they lived, when they were born and died. But sitting at a desk day after day can be a little monotonous, however important the material you find, and a change might be very welcome.

This book is intended to help you make use of a resource which is freely available, and furthermore out in the open air. Family graves in churchyards, chapel burial grounds, and public cemeteries can be a valuable source of information, with inscriptions often full of detail. The names of those buried, when they died and their age at death, where they lived, what their social status was, family connections, references to other family members buried elsewhere.

This may seem rather obvious, and straightforward. As long as you know enough to track down the relevant churchyard or burial ground, the task is simple. However, if your family is from Wales, there is potentially a complication. Many of these gravestones are written in Welsh, and if you are not a fluent Welsh speaker, this may cause difficulties!

It is very frustrating to find what is clearly the right gravestone, with the right name there in the middle of the inscription, but not to be able to read what is said. All that effort wasted – at least until you can find someone to translate. That will mean transcribing what is written there, no easy task if you don't understand the wording and can't be sure of some of the letters where the stone is worn and unclear. How much more rewarding to read the Welsh inscription for yourself, and to understand immediately what it says.

This book is intended to help with the task of reading Welsh inscriptions. It will introduce the words and expressions used, give the English equivalent, and explain any complications you may need to watch out for. Imagine you are faced with an inscription like the one below. You know that it is relevant to your researches because you recognise the names James Morgan, Margaret Morgan and Owen Morgan and the date 1864 looks about right, but the rest of it is a complete mystery. What does all this mean? How can you disentangle the various elements in the flow of the inscription and understand what happened?

Er Cof am
Owen
mab James a Margaret Morgan
o'r plwyf hwn
a fu farw
3 Gorffennaf 1864
yn 34 oed
mewn tanchwa
yng nglofa Cwm Du
Athro ffyddlon yn Ysgol Sul Horeb

In the chapters that follow we will work through the layout of Welsh inscriptions like this, taking each element in turn, and translating as we go along. You should be able by then to read the Welsh and know that what it says is:

In Memory of
Owen
the son of James and Margaret Morgan
from this parish
who died
3 July 1864
aged 34
in an explosion
in Cwm Du colliery
A faithful teacher in Horeb Sunday School

Using a Welsh dictionary

The core task here is of course to understand the meaning of the Welsh words used in the inscription. Looking at the sample inscription above, what does a word like **plwyf** mean? What is the English equivalent? The answer may be straightforward. You get hold of a Welsh-English dictionary, look it up, and find that **plwyf** means *parish*. At the end of this book you will find a short word list, giving translations of the most common words found in inscriptions like this, but you may need to consult a standard Welsh-English dictionary if the inscription turns out to contain words and phrases which are less usual.

This seems simple enough at first glance. Unfortunately, however, there is a problem – one you need to be aware of, though it can be dealt with quite easily when you realise what is going on. The difficulty is that the rules of Welsh grammar sometimes change the first letter of a word, and so the word can look very different depending on what it is doing in the sentence. For instance, the word **plwyf**, meaning *parish*, can appear in its basic form and be easy to find in the dictionary, as it was in the example above. But it could equally well appear in very different guises:

o blwyf Llanelli	*from (the) parish (of) Llanelli*
ym mhlwyf Cenarth	*in (the) parish (of) Cenarth*
a phlwyf Llangollen	*and (the) parish (of) Llangollen*

You won't find forms like **blwyf**, **mhlwyf** or **phlwyf** in the dictionary, even though they are common in real life. The dictionary assumes you know how to backtrack from them to the basic form **plwyf**, which is what you will find there. So how can you work out whether a word you have found in the inscription is a basic form, which *will* appear in the dictionary, or one of these changed forms, which won't?

As we work through the various phrases which appear in an inscription, the core words will be given first in their basic form, as they appear in the dictionary. You will meet a form like **plwyf** (*parish*) in its basic form first. We will then look at the phrases where these words normally appear, and if the first letter has changed, the word will be underlined. This is a warning, reminding you that the word as it appears has been changed from the basic form you would find in the word list at the end of the book, or in a more general dictionary.

o <u>blwyf</u> Llanelli	*from (the) parish (of) Llanelli*
ym <u>mhlwyf</u> Cenarth	*in (the) parish (of) Cenarth*
a <u>phlwyf</u> Llangollen	*and (the) parish (of) Llangollen*

The rules which change the first letter of a word in Welsh in this way are known as Mutation Rules, and the changed forms are often referred to as mutated forms. As a further help, Chapter 14 at the end of the book contains a summary of the letters which change in this way, and how they change. It will also give a set of guidelines showing you how to backtrack from a mutated form to the basic form, which you can then check in the word list.

One other thing to bear in mind is that the appearance of a word may vary because of the way spelling conventions have changed over the years. For instance, the word for *July* may appear as **Gorffennaf** as in the sample inscription shown above, or it may equally well appear as **Gorphennaf** or **Gorphenhaf**. Where there are a number of possible spellings, these will all be given in the word list at the end of the book.

Putting the words together

A further problem you will face in reading the inscriptions relates to the way that individual words are put together to make a sentence. You will be used to the way this is done in English, and may be disconcerted by the fact that Welsh often behaves rather differently.

Going back to the examples just discussed, you will find for instance that words which must appear in the English, are "missing" in the Welsh. The English phrase *the parish of Llanelli* must have the words *the* and *of* in order for the whole thing to make sense. They are not needed in the Welsh, which comes across as rather cryptic by English standards.

plwyf Llanelli	*(the) parish (of) Llanelli*

Another phrase in the sample inscription shown above has the words in a different order in English and Welsh. The English phrase a *faithful teacher* will feel normal and natural to an English-speaker. The Welsh equivalent **athro ffyddlon** has the same meaning, but is set out differently.

athro ffyddlon	*(a) teacher faithful.*

In Welsh there is no word at the beginning corresponding to the English *a*, and the words *teacher* and *faithful* appear in the opposite order to the way they come in the English. You will gradually get used to differences of this kind, and they will be pointed out as they arise in the course of the book.

Reading the words

As you begin to read these inscriptions and try to understand what they mean, you will also find it useful to know how to read them out in Welsh, what they should sound like. Partly for your own satisfaction, but also so that you can ask a Welsh-speaker for help in working out what something means. The spelling conventions of Welsh are rather different to those of English, and reading out a Welsh word as if it were an English one will just cause confusion.

Here is the Welsh alphabet, and the sounds which correspond to each letter. For convenience, these are given in terms of the nearest equivalent in English. In a few cases there is no English equivalent, and the best way forward would be to ask someone to demonstrate this sound for you.

	Nearest English equivalent
a	'a' in *can* or in *father*
b	'b' in *brother*
c	always hard, like 'c' in *can* or 'k' in *kettle*
ch	'ch' in the Scottish word *loch*
d	'd' in *dark*
dd	'th' in *that*
e	'e' in *went*
f	'v' in *van*
ff	'f' in *feather*
g	always hard, like 'g' in *garden*
ng	'ng' in *sing*, occasionally like 'ng' in *finger*

h	'h' in *hat*
i	'ee' in *meet*, or 'i' in *hit*
l	'l' in *lad*
ll	no English equivalent, a breathed 'l', ask someone to demonstrate
m	'm' in *mother*
n	'n' in *nephew*
o	'o' in *lot*
p	'p' in *part*
ph	'f' in *feather*
r	'r' in *rose*
rh	no English equivalent, a breathed 'r', ask someone to demonstrate
s	's' in *sister*
t	't' in *today*
th	'th' in *think*
u	no English equivalent, ask someone to demonstrate
w	'u' in *put* or 'oo' in *mood*
y	two different sounds; like the Welsh letter **u** (see above) if it is in the last syllable of a word; like 'u' in *cup* if it is in any other syllable, or in a few exceptional words like **y** *(the)* and **yn** *(in)*.

There is officially no letter **j** in Welsh, though it shows up in some names like **John** and **Jones**, which come originally from English. Nor is there a **v** in Welsh now, though occasionally old-fashioned spelling conventions may use **v** as English does. The English letters **k**, **q**, **x** and **z** are not used at all.

Two more useful points. Some words are spelled with an accent, as in **môr** (*sea*), but this just means that the letter marked with the accent is long.

The spelling system does not show where the stress comes in a word, as this is normally predictable and comes on the last syllable but one. In a word like **coffadwriaeth** (*memory*), for instance, it will come on the syllable shown here underlined.

Here are some examples of Welsh words which will appear in the inscriptions, and how they sound, using the conventions outlined above:

bu farw	*died*	bee varoo
hunodd	*fell asleep*	heenoth
claddwyd	*was buried*	klathooeed

Showing respect and taking care

Churchyards, burial grounds and cemeteries are all sacred ground. Be respectful at all times. Don't leave litter or make a loud noise, and be careful when you park not to obstruct other people's access. If there is a noticeboard, be sure to follow any instructions listed.

Treat the gravestones with care and don't pull away ivy or scrape off lichen and moss. You may cause further damage to the stone by doing this. You will be surprised how much of the wording you can read just by moving into a different position, or tracing the carved words gently with your finger tip. Remember that most gravestones face east, and it is usually easier to read them in the morning as the sun shines directly on the inscription. If the sun is shining from behind the stone, your eyes will be dazzled, and it will be much more difficult to make out the wording. A dull cloudy day is better in fact than bright sun for this kind of work. Taking photographs for your own use is usually acceptable, though it would be a good idea to inform the church or chapel authorities as a matter of courtesy.

If you find a gate shut when you arrive, shut it again behind you, to prevent stock wandering in and causing damage. If a gate is locked, then you will need to get permission to go in from the relevant church or chapel authorities, or from the local council. It may have been locked to prevent vandalism, and in this case permission will usually be given to someone with a genuine reason for wanting to gain access. If it has been locked because there is a safety issue, you may not be able to enter. It is always possible that the local family history society may have a transcript of the inscriptions: not as good as seeing the gravestone yourself, but better than nothing.

Watch out for uneven ground, trailing brambles, and stones hidden by grass or other growth. It is very easy to slip or stumble. Wear strong shoes or boots, and suitable clothing. Don't try and move stones which have fallen, and be careful of those which are leaning and unstable. In some churchyards the authorities have taped off certain areas as unsafe – respect these tapes and stay away, however frustrating this may be.

One important though unpleasant fact to bear in mind: you may occasionally, in a cemetery which has become neglected and overgrown, find such objects as broken glass or discarded needles. Be careful, and if you find anything you consider dangerous, report it to the responsible authorities.

It is a good idea to take someone else with you, partly so that you have company and help in carrying out the search, but also as a precaution in case something does go wrong and you twist an ankle or have some other mishap. If you are in a lonely or inaccessible location, out of mobile coverage, you will be glad of the backup. Finally, if you ever feel uneasy and uncomfortable, particularly if you are alone, trust your instincts and leave. You can always come back, with company, and have another go. I hope that this will not happen to you, but it is better to be alert to the possibility than caught unawares.

1

'In memory of ...'

Most inscriptions start with a phrase which sets the scene and introduces the name of the person commemorated. In English this would be *In memory of* ... or *Here lies* ..., followed by the name of the person commemorated. In Welsh too there are a number of such phrases, which you will want to understand, if only to be sure that you are dealing here with conventional phrases rather than important factual evidence. These fall broadly into three different types.

Er cof am ... *(In memory of ...)*

This form is perhaps the simplest type of introductory phrase, and can be literally translated into English as *In memory of.* The word **cof** *(memory)* is sometimes replaced by other similar forms which are used in exactly the same way. Sometimes the form **er** is left out. This does not change the meaning:

(er) cof am	*(in) memory of*
(er) coffadwriaeth am	*(in) memory of*
(er) coffhad am	*(in) memory of*
(er) coffa am	*(in) memory of*
(er) cofiant am	*(in) memory of*
cofion am	*memories of*
atgofion am	*memories of*

A more flowery style is common, however, specifying what kind of memory is involved, usually loving or respectful according to the conventions of the age and the nature of family relationships.

The words added may include the following:

annwyl	*dear, beloved*
anwylaf	*dearest, most beloved*
anrhydeddus	*honourable*
caredig	*loving, kind*
cariadus	*loving*
cu	*beloved*
cysegredig	*sacred*
da	*good*
dwys	*grave, serious*
hapus	*happy*
hiraethus	*full of longing*
hyfryd	*lovely*
melys	*sweet*
parchus	*respectful*
serchog	*loving*
serchus	*loving*
tyner	*tender*

These may come before **cof** as they would in English, or they may follow. The meaning is the same, but notice that the first letter of **cof** will change if it comes second:

er cof parchus am	*in respectful memory of*
er cof serchus am	*in loving memory of*
er parchus gof am	*in respectful memory of*
er serchus gof am	*in loving memory of*

More recent inscriptions sometimes have a slightly modified version of this introduction, with the word **cofio** *(to remember)*. This form too may be elaborated, using the same words as before, though with an intervening **yn** or **'n** in the Welsh which turns *respectful* or *loving* into *respectfully* or *lovingly*:

i gofio	*to remember*
i gofio'n barchus	*to remember respectfully*
i gofio'n annwyl	*to remember lovingly*

Other related expressions do appear, though they are not very common:

cysegredig i goffadwriaeth	*sacred to the memory (of)*
atgof uwch angof	*recollection above forgetfulness*
atgo serch	*recollections of love*

Yma y gorwedd *(Here lies)*

Another set of introductory expressions has a rather more old fashioned feel, and they are again straightforward to translate. These correspond broadly to the English *Here lies*. Other words or longer phrases are sometimes used instead of **yma** (*here*), or may indeed be used alongside **yma**:

yma	y gorwedd	*here lies*
isod	y gorwedd	*below lies*
goris	y gorwedd	*below lies*
odditanodd	y gorwedd	*below lies*
yma isod	y gorwedd	*here below lies*
dyma lle	y gorwedd	*here is where lies*
dyma'r fan	y gorwedd	*here is the place lies*
dyma'r fan lle	y gorwedd	*here is the place where lies*
wele'r fan lle	y gorwedd	*behold the place where lies*

And instead of **gorwedd** (*lies*) we find another range of possibilities:

yma y gorwedd	*here lies*
yma y cysga	*here sleeps*
yma y gorffwys	*here rests*
yma yr huna	*here sleeps*
yma y claddwyd	*here was buried*
yma y daearwyd	*here was laid in earth*
yma y dodwyd	*here was laid*
yma y gosodwyd	*here was laid*
yma y rhoddwyd	*here was laid*

These phrases may be followed straightforwardly by the name of the person commemorated, but it is common too for there to be a further element before the name, as in the English *Here lies the body of:*

corff	*body*	
cyrff	*bodies (of several people)*	
gweddillion daearol	*earthly remains*	lit. *remains earthly*
gweddillion marwol	*mortal remains*	lit. *remains mortal*
rhan ddaearol	*earthly part*	lit. *part earthly*
rhan farwol	*mortal part*	lit. *part mortal*
yr hyn oedd farwol	*that which was mortal*	
yr hyn sydd farwol	*that which is mortal*	

Note that the order of words is different here in the Welsh and English, so that a literal translation of **gweddillion daearol** is actually *remains earthly*. The meaning is the same.

Combining these various options gives phrases such as the following. Here some of the words needed in the English, such as *the* and *of,* are missing in the Welsh, though the meaning is the same:

yma y gorwedd corff	*here lies (the) body (of)*
yma y gorwedd gweddillion daearol	*here lie (the) earthly remains (of)*
isod y claddwyd rhan farwol	*beneath was buried (the) mortal part (of)*

A slightly different version of this introduction is also found from time to time:

yma mae'n gorwedd	*here is lying*
yma mae'n gorphwys	*here is resting*
gorphwyso yma mae	*resting here is*
huno yma mae	*sleeping here is*

Bedd *(The) Grave (of)*

A third type of introductory phrase is less common and rather more cryptic, merely noting that this is the grave of the person commemorated. This can be simply translated as *(The) Grave (of)*, and here again the words *the* and *of* which are needed in the English are not present in the Welsh. A range of other words can be used in the same way:

bedd	*grave*
arwylfaen	*funerary stone*
beddfaen	*gravestone*
bedd-lech	*gravestone*
beddrod	*grave*
carreg	*stone*

claddfa	*burial place*
cofadail	*memorial*
cofeb	*memorial*
cofgolofn	*memorial column*
gorffwysfa	*resting place*
gorweddle	*resting place*
gorweddfa	*resting place*
gwyddfa	*burial place*
hunfan	*sleeping place*
maen	*stone*

Or one of these words may appear in a slightly longer phrase:

dyma fedd	*here is (the) grave (of)*
llyma fedd	*here is (the) grave (of)*
wele fedd	*behold (the) grave (of)*

Complex forms

In some cases these various introductory formulae are combined to give longer and more complicated phrases. Combining the first two types outlined above gives forms such as these:

er coffadwriaeth mai	*in memory that*
yma y claddwyd	*here was buried ...*
er coffadwriaeth mai	*in memory that*
dyma lle y gorwedd	*here is where lies....*

Adding in the third type gives even longer phrases, such as these:

codwyd y garreg hon	*this stone was raised*
er coffadwriaeth mai	*in memory that*
yma y claddwyd	*here was buried ...*

gosodwyd y maen hwn	*this stone was placed*
er coffadwriaeth mai	*in memory that*
dyma lle y gorwedd	*here is where lies ...*
y beddfaen hwn a noda	*this gravestone records*
yr amser a'r lle y claddwyd	*the time and the place was buried ...*

It is not possible here to list all the possible variations which may appear, but you should be able to disentangle the main elements using the various formulae given above.

Now try these:

See if you can translate the wording shown in these photographs, using the phrases explained in this section. (Answers on page 26.)

1.

2.

3.

4.

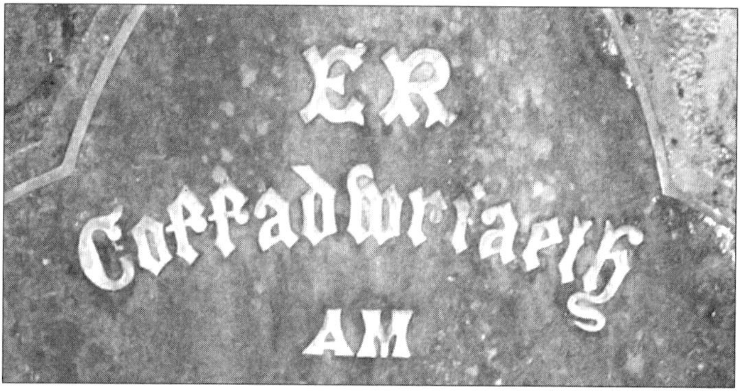

Answers: *1: in loving memory of; 2: in loving memory of; 3: here lies (the) earthly part (of); 4 in memory of*

Wills and Gravestones

Who decides how the inscription on a gravestone will read? I had always assumed that this was a matter for the family, and that the wording we see gives us some insight into their feelings as they mourn the person commemorated here. But not every time, it seems. I recently, quite by accident, came across a case where the person commemorated had chosen his own epitaph before his death, and there it is indeed on his gravestone, just as he had decreed.

I was reading through a collection of wills held in the National Library of Wales, when I noticed that one of these specified the form which the gravestone should take and what the wording on it should be. Thomas Williams, also known as Gwilym Morgannwg, was from Llanwonno near Pontypridd, and died in 1835. He wanted a rough stone pillar set up, with the following wording:

/ | \
Yma gorwedd
Gwilym Morgannwg
bu farw y ...
yn ... oed
18 ...
[Here lies / Gwilym Morgannwg /
he died the ... / aged ... / 18 ...]

This was interesting in itself, but even more so as I felt sure that I had actually seen this inscription in one of the local churchyards. Back to my notes, and another visit to check, and there it was in the churchyard at Llanfabon, not far away. Clearly his wishes had been respected, the inscription set out almost exactly as he had asked.

/ | \
Yma gorwedd
Gwilym
Morgannwg
bu farw
Awst y 13 1835
yn 56 oed
[Here / lies / Gwilym / Morgannwg /
he died / August the 13 1835 / aged 56]

Since then I have found other cases where the will sets out in detail what should appear in the inscription, and it may well be worth checking whether this has happened at some point in your own family. There might be a clue here to an unexpected line of research.

Here, for instance, we find the symbol / | \ in the inscription. This is usually associated with the growth of interest in bardic activity and druidism in the nineteenth century, and suggests that he was part of this movement. The fact that his name is given as Gwilym Morgannwg rather than as William Thomas reinforces this view, the bardic name being more important to him than his everyday identity. Would the family have chosen to commemorate him like this, or would they have chosen a more conventional form of words? As it is we can follow up the hints in the inscription, and be grateful for them.

2

Personal names

These introductory phrases are usually followed by the name of the person commemorated in the inscription. In most cases this is very straightforward, and even where the wording is in Welsh the name is immediately recognisable. It is worth bearing in mind, however, that occasionally the name may not be quite what you were expecting.

First names

One problem is that the actual form of the name may vary. Many first names come in two guises, a formal official version which is what we find in parish records and official documents, and an informal Welsh version reflecting normal, everyday usage. The same man may have been known as **Evan** or as **Ifan**, depending on the situation. The same woman may have been known as **Margaret** or **Marged**, again depending on the situation. It is usually the official version that will appear on a gravestone, but sometimes in a Welsh-language inscription we find the informal version. If the name in the inscription looks slightly different to what you were expecting, it is worth checking if this is just an alternative Welsh spelling for a name you have only come across in its official form. Equally the inscription may have the official version of a name you have only met previously in its natural, Welsh form. Here are some of the most common variants:

	Official	Informal
Men	David	Dafydd, Dai
	Evan	Ifan
	Howell	Hywel
	Hugh	Huw
	James	Siâms, Jâms
	Jenkin	Siencyn
	John	Ioan, Ieuan, Siôn
	Rees	Rhys
	Richard	Rhisiart
	Thomas	Tomos
	William	Gwilym
Women	Catherine	Catrin
	Elizabeth	Lisa, Betsan, Bet
	Jane	Siân
	Janet	Sioned
	Margaret	Marged
	Mary	Mari, Mair

Family names

Family names may vary too, and again the form you find in the inscription may not be quite what you were expecting. Family names in the modern sense are a comparatively late development in Wales, and a certain amount of confusion and inconsistency shows up in various forms of documentation, including the inscriptions on gravestones. The 'same' family name may appear in various different forms, and while most families today have adopted one of these as a consistent usage, this was not always the case in the past. More than one form may well have been used at different times by the same family, even by the same individual.

Many of the family names found in Welsh are what are called patronymics. Traditionally a son's first name would be followed by his father's name. **Morgan** the son of **John** would be known as **Morgan John**; in the next generation **David** the son of **Morgan** would be known as **David Morgan**, and so on. The picture shifts in each generation, and there is no family name as such:

John Griffith
|
Morgan John
|
David Morgan

Gradually this custom died out, and whatever second name happened to be in use at this point became fossilised as a family name, used consistently from then on by the family, from one generation to another. It might, for instance, have happened in the family illustrated here if **David Morgan**'s son **Owen** did not follow the old pattern, but held onto **Morgan**, which from then on functioned as a family name in the sense that we understand this:

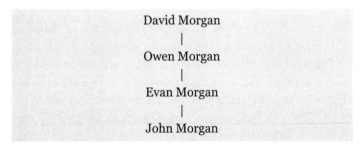

David Morgan
|
Owen Morgan
|
Evan Morgan
|
John Morgan

These family names may appear in exactly the same form as the original Christian name, as **Morgan** in the example shown above, for instance. There is however another option where **s** is added at the end, and the same person may use both **Morgan** and **Morgans** as a surname at different times. They do not seem to have been seen as 'different' family names. In some cases adding the **s** leads to further changes in the name, so that **John** for instance becomes **Jones**, and again the same person may use both **John** and **Jones**. Some of the most common examples of this are shown below.

David	Davies
Edward	Edwards
Evan	Evans
Gruffydd, Griffith, Gruffudd	Griffiths
Jenkin	Jenkins
John	Jones
Morgan	Morgans
Reynold	Reynolds
Walter	Walters
Watkin	Watkins
William	Williams

Where the original name ends in **s**, as with **James** or **Thomas**, there is only one form and no scope for variation of this kind.

Traces of the traditional system, with the name changing in each generation, do sometimes show up on gravestones in the eighteenth century and even later. I have seen cases where the inscription on a family grave commemorates for instance first the father, **John Williams**, and later on his son, **Owen Jones**. Or it may refer to one **Robert Jones**, the son of **John Owen**.

There is no mistake here. The inscription is merely following the old Welsh system, and dates from a time where the family had not yet adopted a stable family name.

More Family Names

Some names have a third option, which reflects even more clearly the traditional pattern of naming. The Welsh word for *son* is **mab**, and originally this would have been included in the full form of the name. The word **mab** (*son*) was abbreviated to give **ab** before a vowel, **ap** before **r** or **h**, as in these examples:

Morgan mab Owen	Morgan ab Owen	*Morgan son (of) Owen*
Thomas mab Rhys	Thomas ap Rhys	*Thomas son (of) Rhys*
Ellis mab Hugh	Ellis ap Hugh	*Ellis son (of) Hugh*

When eventually stable family names developed, the **b** of **ab** or the **p** of **ap** stuck to the following name, and so **ab Owen** became **Bowen, ap Rhys** became **Prys** or **Price**, and **ap Hugh** became **Pugh**. The other options already discussed were also available, giving three choices. Again there may be confusion, with the same family, or even the same person, using these various forms at different times:

Bellis	Ellis	
Bevan	Evan	Evans
Beynon	Eynon	
Bowen	Owen	Owens
Parry	Harry	Harries
Penry	Henry	
Powell	Howell	Howells
Prys, Price, Breese	Rees, Rice	

Pritchard	Richard	Richards
Probert	Robert	Roberts
Prosser	Rosser, Roger	Rogers
Pugh, Puw	Hugh, Huw	Hughes

In comparatively recent times, some families have made a deliberate choice to use an **ab/ap** form, even though they had not done so for many generations. Where the family, for instance, had been known as **Howells** or **Powell**, they have begun to use **ap Hywel**. When you find an unexpected form of this kind in an inscription, it is worth checking if this has happened in the family you are researching.

Women

The discussion of family names so far has been in terms of men, fathers and sons, because the conventions which developed in Wales were essentially patriarchal. If we go back to the traditional system, just as a son was known as **mab Owen** (*son (of) Owen*), a daughter was known as **ferch Owen** (*daughter (of) Owen*), with both being identified in terms of who the father was. As the old system was gradually abandoned, however, the modern family names which emerged were all based on the male forms, and the female equivalents did not survive to give alternative family names. Women took first their father's family name, and then changed to their husband's family name on marriage.

Interestingly, this does not always happen in the inscriptions. Occasionally when a woman is commemorated, her family name is different from her husband's. Presumably she had in practice retained her own family name on marriage, and was still known in the community by that name. Inscriptions will refer to **Martha Williams** the wife of **John Pritchard**, or to **Mary James** the wife of **John Parry**. There is nothing in these inscriptions to imply that the practice was seen as in any way odd or abnormal. It is unusual, but does occur from time to time and is worth watching out for.

Other family names

Not all family names are patronymics. They may derive from Welsh terms referring to physical characteristics, or less often occupations. Here are a few examples:

Gwynn, Wynne, Wyn	gwyn	*white, fair*
Lloyd, Floyd	llwyd	*grey*
Moyle, Voyle	moel	*bald*
Vaughan	bychan	*small, younger*
Saer	saer	*carpenter*

Others derive rather from placenames - **Mostyn, Pennant, Lougher, Roach**. Or they may not be in origin Welsh names at all, but rather names which were brought into Wales by some distant ancestor who came here from England, France or further afield. Names of this kind, which are common in Wales, are **Bonsall, Coslett, Devonald, Havard, Jarman, Scourfield,** and **Wigley**. And many more, including as I am only too aware, **Awbery**. If you are interested in how surnames developed in Wales, what they mean, and in which areas they appear most commonly, have a look at the reference books listed in Chapter 16, which explore this whole area in more detail.

The Change from Welsh to English

Many families in Wales were originally Welsh-speaking, but today speak only English, and it is interesting to ask when this change actually occurred in each case. Did it happen early on, some time in the nineteenth century? Or did the family continue to speak Welsh until quite recently? The language of the gravestones can often help us work out what happened.

We often find a gravestone where the first part of the inscription is in Welsh, but then suddenly there is a change and later additions are all in English. Here is an example from the burial ground of Old Moriah chapel in Risca, not far from Newport. The first person commemorated was Catherine Llewelyn and the details of her death are all in Welsh. When her husband died in 1889, the new material was all added in English. Not only that, but his name appears differently in the two parts of the inscription. In the first part his Christian name is given in its Welsh form as **Iago**, but afterwards it appears in the corresponding English form as **James**.

Er cof am Catherine Gwraig Iago Llewelyn
Dilledydd o'r Plwyf hwn
yr hon a fu farw Gorph 11 1837 yn 41 oed

[In memory of Catherine the wife of Iago Llewelyn
Draper of this Parish who died July 11 1837 aged 41.]

In loving memory of the above James Llewelyn
who died May 6 1889
and was enterred at Bethesda Ceven

How can we interpret this? It seems likely that both Catherine and Iago/James Llewelyn were Welsh-speaking. When Catherine died, her husband quite naturally arranged for the inscription to be carved in Welsh. When he died, over fifty years later, there was no one to add the appropriate Welsh phrases and so he is commemorated in English. Catherine and Iago/James had probably, like many people in those days, decided not to pass on the language to their children, who would have grown up with little or no Welsh, certainly not enough to deal with the demands of a formal inscription on a gravestone. The family was now, to all intents and purposes, English-speaking.

This is, of course, only the first step and we would need to look for other information with a bearing on the language used in the family at different times. It does, however, suggest when the language shift may have happened, so that we can focus our efforts on the period most likely to be relevant.

3

Family relationships

We now move into the part of the inscription where there will be genuine information about the person commemorated. This will in most cases include information about family relationships, and may involve reference to the family into which the person commemorated was born, to their husband or wife, and/or to their wider extended family.

The immediate family

This first set of words relates to the immediate family, the parents and children, the brothers and sisters, the husband and wife:

tad	*father*
mam	*mother*
rhiant, rhieni	*parent, parents*
mab, meibion	*son, sons*
bachgen, bechgyn	*son, sons*
merch, merched	*daughter, daughters*
geneth, genethod	*daughter, daughters (north Wales)*
plentyn, plant	*child, children*
baban, babanod	*baby, babies (of either gender)*
maban, mabanod	*baby, babies (of either gender)*
brawd, brodyr	*brother, brothers*
chwaer, chwiorydd	*sister, sisters*

gefell, gefeilliaid	*twin, twins*
gŵr	*husband*
gwraig	*wife*
priod	*spouse (used for either the husband or the wife)*
gweddw	*widow*
diweddar	*late*

These words do not usually stand alone, but appear in phrases which make clear what the relationship is in detail. Here are some examples:

mab John a Mary Evans	*(the) son (of) John and Mary Evans*
merch Owen a Hannah Jones	*(the) daughter (of) Owen and Hannah Jones*
plant James a Margaret Miles	*(the) children (of) James and Margaret Miles*
gŵr Ann Morgan	*(the) husband (of) Ann Morgan*
gwraig Llywelyn John	*(the) wife (of) Llywelyn John*
gweddw Evan James	*(the) widow (of) Evan James*

A word such as *son* or *daughter* will appear first, followed by the names of the parents. In the same way, the word *husband, wife* or *widow* will appear first, followed by the name of the wife or husband respectively. As usual, the words *the* and *of* are needed in the English, but not in the Welsh. Where the person commemorated was a widow, the phrase **y diweddar** (*the late*) will often appear before the name of the husband.

gweddw y diweddar Evan James	*(the) widow (of) the late Evan James*

Where children are commemorated, two other conventional types of wording are sometimes found. In the second, instead of the expected phrase, with both parents given equal prominence, we find the focus on the father, with the wife only mentioned in second place:

mab i John a Mary Evans	*son to John and Mary Evans*
merch i Owen a Hannah Jones	*daughter to Owen and Hannah Jones*
plant i James a Margaret Miles	*children to James and Margaret Miles*
mab John Evans o Mary ei wraig	*(the) son (of) John Evans by Mary his wife*
mab John Evans o'i wraig Mary	*(the) son (of) John Evans by his wife Mary*

A Modern Variant

A form of words found in comparatively recent inscriptions uses the words *my* and *our* rather than spelling out the relationship:

fy	*my*
ein	*our*

Examples of this are:

fy annwyl wraig, Olwen	*my beloved wife, Olwen*
fy mhriod annwyl, Hywel	*my beloved spouse, Hywel*
ein rhieni, John a Hannah Jones	*our parents, John and Hannah Jones*

ein hannwyl ferch, Mari	*our beloved daughter, Mari*

The wider family

There are also from time to time references to the wider, extended family in these inscriptions.

taid	*grandfather (north Wales)*
tadcu	*grandfather (south Wales)*
nain	*grandmother (north Wales)*
mamgu	*grandmother (south Wales)*
hen daid	*great-grandfather (north Wales)*
hen dadcu	*great-grandfather (south Wales)*
hen nain	*great-grandmother (north Wales)*
hen famgu	*great-grandmother (south Wales)*
ŵyr	*grandson*
wyres	*granddaughter*
wyrion	*grandchildren*
wyresau	*granddaughters*
gor-ŵyr	*great-grandson*
gor-wyres	*great-grand-daughter*
gor-wyrion	*great-grandchildren*
ewythr	*uncle*
modryb	*aunt*
nai	*nephew*
nith	*niece*
cefnder	*cousin (male)*
cyfnither	*cousin (female)*
tad-yng-nghyfraith	*father-in-law*
mam-yng-nghyfraith	*mother-in-law*

mab-yng-nghyfraith	*son-in-law*
merch-yng-nghyfraith	*daughter-in-law*
brawd-yng-nghyfraith	*brother-in-law*
chwaer-yng-nghyfraith	*sister-in-law*

Even in the days before divorce was widely accepted, the loss of a husband or wife often led to remarriage, and complex family relationships did exist, so that another set of forms proves relevant:

ail ŵr	*second husband*
ail wraig	*second wife*
llysdad	*stepfather*
llysfam	*stepmother*
llysfab	*stepson*
llysferch	*stepdaughter*
mab mabwysiedig	*adopted son*
merch fabwysiedig	*adopted daughter*
mab maeth	*foster son*
merch faeth	*foster daughter*

It is also worth bearing in mind in this context that the terms given above for 'in-law' relationships are sometimes used to mean rather a 'step' relationship. Which meaning is intended in a particular case can be resolved only be comparing the wording of the inscription with other material you may have found.

tad-yng-nghyfraith	*stepfather*
mam-yng-nghyfraith	*stepmother*
mab-yng-nghyfraith	*stepson*
merch-yng-nghyfraith	*stepdaughter*

Two further very general terms also appear sometimes in this context:

teulu	*family*
perthnasau	*relatives*

Now try these:

See if you can translate the wording shown in these photographs, using the phrases explained in this section. (Answers below)

1.

2.

3.

4.

Answers: 1: (the) son (of) *John and Rachel Williams;*
2: (the) *daughter (of) the late David and Eliza Williams;*
3: (my) *father and mother;* 4:(the) *wife (of) David Davies*

Children dying young

It's one thing to read in general terms about high rates of infant mortality in the past, quite another to see the reality. So often these gravestones commemorate a young child, or indeed several children from the same family. We can hardly imagine the experience of losing child after child to illnesses which would today be so easily overcome.

The factual details are stoic, usually giving only the child's name and age, and the date of death. It is in the poems which follow that the grief and sorrow of the parents can at last appear. Here one picture appears time and again - the child as a flower which blooms only for a short time in this world, and is then taken to bloom for ever in paradise. An image summing up the beauty and brevity of life, found throughout Wales in many forms but carrying the same message.

Fel blodeuyn yn ymagor
Ydoedd yma gyda ni
Ond llaw ddwyfol a'i trawsblanodd
I'r baradwys nefol fry.

Like a flower opening
She was here with us
But a divine hand transplanted her
To the heavenly paradise above.

The flower may be a rose, or a lily, symbolising the beauty and innocence of the child.

Megis rhosyn y blodeuodd,
Megis rhosyn buan gwywodd
Ond daw bore gwynfydedig
Y blodeua'n anllygredig.

Like a rose he flowered
Like a rose he swiftly faded
But a blessed morning will come
When he will flower incorruptibly.

Cipiodd angel Rachel hawddgar
Oddiwrthym ato ef
Gwywai'r lili ar y ddaear
Er mwyn gwynu yn y nef.

An angel took lovely Rachel
From us to him
The lily faded on the earth
To bloom in heaven.

These poems are perhaps all an echo of Biblical verses such as "Dyddiau dyn sydd fel glaswelltyn: megis blodeuyn y maes felly y blodeua efe" *[As for man, his days are as grass: as a flower of the field, so he flourisheth]* Psalm 103.15. A community so well versed in the Bible would naturally turn to it in the search for a way of expressing their deepest feelings.

4

More about the family

The inscriptions in fact often tell us more about the place of the person who is commemorated in the family. They may specify, for instance, if he or she was the oldest or the youngest in the family, or the second or third, or perhaps the only son, daughter or child.

bach, bychan	*little*
cyntaf	*first*
hynaf	*oldest*
ieuengaf, ifancaf	*youngest*
olaf	*last*
ail	*second*
trydydd	*third*
unig	*only*

The words for *little, first, oldest, youngest* and *last* will follow the word describing the relationship, but the others will always come first:

mab hynaf	*oldest son*
merch ieuengaf	*youngest daughter*
ail fab	*second son*
trydydd mab	*third son*
unig blentyn	*only child*

The words **bach** or **bychan** (*little*) are used in two different ways. They may be used simply to stress how young the child was, or when used of a *brother* or *sister* the meaning is rather *younger*:

mab bach John a Mary Evans	(the) little son (of) John and Mary Evans
chwaer fach Dewi	(the) little sister (of) Dewi

At other times the focus is on the number of children in the family. Several children, for instance, may be buried in the same grave, a sad situation but one which was common in the days of high infant mortality and the lack of medical treatment for the usual childhood illnesses. There are two different ways to express number in Welsh, and although they look different, the meaning is identical. The number may come first, followed by whatever is being counted. Or the number may be followed by the word **o** (*of*) and then whatever is being counted:

dau fab	*two sons*	*lit. two son*
dwy ferch	*two daughters*	*lit. two daughter*
dau blentyn	*two children*	*lit. two child*
dau faban	*two babies*	*lit. two baby*
dau o feibion	*two sons*	*lit. two of sons*
dwy o ferched	*two daughters*	*lit. two of daughters*
dau o blant	*two children*	*lit. two of children*
dau o fabanod	*two babies*	*lit. two of babies*

The numbers you are likely to find are listed below. It seems unlikely that in this context you will need to go further than *ten*, even allowing for the high birth rate and large families of the past!

You will see from the list below that some of the numbers have several different forms. We find **dau** (*two*), **tri** (*three*) and **pedwar** (*four*) where there is a group either of men or boys or a group of mixed sex; we find **dwy** (*two*), **tair** (*three*) and **pedair** (*four*) where there is a group of women or girls. Other numbers such as **pump/pum** (*five*), **chwech/chwe** (*six*) and **deg/deng** (*ten*) have different forms depending on which word follows. You do not need to worry about this, just bear in mind that these different forms are the 'same' word:

un	*one*
dau	*two (men or boys, or group of mixed sex)*
dwy	*two (women or girls only)*
tri	*three (men or boys, or group of mixed sex)*
tair	*three (women or girls only)*
pedwar	*four (men or boys, or group of mixed sex)*
pedair	*four (women or girls only)*
pump, pum	*five*
chwech, chwe	*six*
saith	*seven*
wyth	*eight*
naw	*nine*
deg, deng	*ten*

A loving father

This section of the inscription is rarely a simple catalogue of the family relationships involved. Very often the description stresses the fact that the person commemorated was loving and beloved. These are some of the words which frequently appear, used of both men and women:

addfwyn	*tender*
annwyl	*dear, beloved*
cariadus	*loving*
caredig	*loving, kind*
cymwys	*worthy*

ffyddlon	*faithful*
gofalus	*caring*
hawddgar	*beloved*
hoff	*beloved*
hoffus	*beloved*
hynaws	*kind, loving*
rhinweddol	*virtuous*
tyner	*tender*

Some of them can appear either before or after the word for *mother*, *father* or other family member:

annwyl briod, priod annwyl	*(a) beloved spouse*
hoff dadcu, tadcu hoff	*(a) beloved grandfather*

Others more often appear following this word:

tad gofalus	*(a) caring father*
mam ofalus	*(a) caring mother*
tadcu cariadus	*(a) loving grandfather*
mamgu gariadus	*(a) loving grandmother*

Occasionally the description will be longer, with more than one word used to praise the departed, or more than one of his or her roles within the family highlighted.

tad cariadus a thyner	*(a) loving and tender father*
mamgu annwyl a gofalus	*(a) beloved and caring grandmother*
priod hoff a mam ofalus	*(a) beloved spouse and caring mother*
tad a thaid annwyl	*(a) beloved father and grandfather*

Other rôles

Other rôles beyond the family are also referred to in many cases, where the person commemorated is praised as a good friend or neighbour:

cyfaill	*friend*
cymydog	*neighbour (male)*
cymdoges	*neighbour (female)*
ffrind	*friend*
ymgeledd	*support*
cyfaill ffyddlon	*(a) faithful friend*
cymydog da	*(a) good neighbour*
ymgeledd cymwys	*(a) worthy support*

Now try these:

See if you can translate the wording shown in these photographs, using the phrases explained in this section. (Answers on page 51.)

1.

2.

3.

4.

Answers: 1.: *(the) beloved wife (of) William Thomas; 2: (a) beloved mother and grandmother; 3: Idris their eldest son; 4: (a) beloved spouse and tender father*

Farewell

Many of the poems in these inscriptions focus on the family, and the need to say farewell. A husband who has died speaks to the wife he has left behind, or it may be that the wife has died first and speaks to her husband. The word **priod** (*spouse*) is used quite naturally in Welsh for either husband or wife, and means that the same poem can be used in either situation.

Ffarwel i ti fy annwyl briod
Fe ddaeth cennad i fy hol
Teithiais lwybr o'r dieithraf
Ni ddychwelaf byth yn ôl.

Farewell to thee my dear spouse
A messenger came to fetch me
I have travelled a strange path
I will never come back.

Parents and children too bid each other farewell, and occasionally even the grandchildren feature.

Ffarwel blant a ffarwel wyron,
Farwel bawb o'n hoff gyfeillion;
Yma'n gorwedd ry'm yn dawel,
Hyd nes bloeddio yr Archangel.

Farewell children and farewell grandchildren
Farewell all of our dear friends;
Here we lie quietly
Till the Archangel shall call out.

Sometimes there is good advice for the children - to love each other and respect God's laws, or an attempt to offer comfort as the dead look ahead to the day when they will all meet again in heaven. The bonds of love are portrayed as unbreakable, even when the family is torn apart by death.

At other times it is the living who speak, mourning their loss at the graveside. Here are parents whose son has died.

Ffarwel fy mab rhaid ymadael
A gadael gand dy fedd
Troi'n cefn er mor anawdd
Heb olwg ar dy wedd.

Farewell my son we must go
And leave thy grave
Turn our back though so hard
With no sight of thy face.

And here a husband who has lost his wife, looking forward in hope of being reunited in heaven.

Ffarwel briod hoff ac anwyl
Ti ddiengaist o fy mla'n
Gobeithio cawn gyfarfod etto
I gyd ganu'r nefol gân.

Farewell my beloved and dear wife
Thou hast escaped before me
Hope we can meet again
To sing the heavenly song together.

5

Where did they live?

Many inscriptions include information, often quite detailed, about where the person commemorated was living. This may include references to a specific farm or house, a parish or town, and the county where this is located.

The house

In a rural area the inscription may just mention the name of the farm or house, and in an urban area may give the address:

Hafod Isaf
Tan y Castell
3 Ffordd y Capel

Or the word **o** (*from*) may come before the name of the house.

o Hafod Isaf	*from Hafod Isaf*
o Dan y Castell	*from Tan y Castell*
o 3 Ffordd y Capel	*from 3 Ffordd y Capel*

It is of course not possible here to list the full range of farm and house names, and it will be necessary to check these against other local sources of information such as maps, documents and talking to people who know the area.

The parish

Traditionally the main reference point in this context is the parish, and most people were buried in the parish where they had lived:

plwyf	*parish*	
y plwyf hwn	*this parish*	lit. *the parish this*
y plwyf yma	*this parish*	lit. *the parish this*

The wording may merely say that someone was from this parish, or give the house or farm name and say that it was located in this parish:

o'r plwyf hwn	*from this parish*
o Hendre yn y plwyf hwn	*from Hendre in this parish*

If the person commemorated was not from the immediate parish, the name of the parish where he or she *did* live will follow the word **plwyf** (*parish*). As usual, the words *the* and *of* are needed in the English but not in the Welsh:

o blwyf Llannon	*from (the) parish (of) Llannon*
o Hendre ym mhlwyf Llannon	*from Hendre in (the) parish (of) Llannon*

Beyond the parish

The parish is not the only reference point for where someone lived, and a number of other forms are found:

pentref	*village*
tref	*town*
treflan	*small town*
dinas	*city*
lle	*place*
swydd	*county*
sir	*county*

As before, the person commemorated may merely be said to have come from this particular village or town or county:

o'r pentref hwn	*from this village*
o'r dref hon	*from this town*
o'r dreflan hon	*from this small town*
o'r lle hwn	*from this place*
o'r swydd hon	*from this county*
o'r sir hon	*from this county*

The name of the village, town or county may be given:

o bentref Brynberian	*from (the) village (of) Brynberian*
o dref Aberystwyth	*from (the) town (of) Aberystwyth*
o sir Fôn	*from (the) county (of) Anglesey*

If the name of a farm or house is given, it will be noted that this is in the village or town mentioned:

o Hendre yn y pentref hwn	*from Hendre in this village*
o Hendre yn y dref hon	*from Hendre in this town*
o Hendre ym mhentref Sarn	*from Hendre in (the) village (of) Sarn*
o Hendre yn nhref Porth	*from Hendre in (the) town (of) Porth*

Sometimes the name of a village or town will appear on its own, with no use of the words for *village* or *town* as such:

o Aberystwyth	*from Aberystwyth*
o Bontypridd	*from Pontypridd*
o Langollen	*from Llangollen*

Occasionally it will be specified that the place referred to is near somewhere else:

ger, gerllaw	*near*
o Hafod Isaf ger y dref hon	*from Hafod Isaf near this town*
o Hafod Isaf gerllaw tref Tywyn	*from Hafod Isaf near (the) town (of) Tywyn*

Welsh and English place-names

Most place-names in Wales are straightforwardly Welsh in origin. The spelling may vary, either because spelling conventions have changed over the years, or because an anglicised spelling has been adopted. You may find **Caerffili**, with the conventional Welsh spelling, or equally **Caerphilly**, with a more English spelling. A place name which begins with **ll** may appear as **Llanidloes**, following normal Welsh conventions, or in an anglicised form as **Lanidloes**. Similarly **Aberdyfi**, with the normal Welsh use of the letter **f**, may also appear as **Aberdovey**, following English spelling conventions. The reverse situation also arises when a place name is actually English in origin, as **Wrexham**, for instance, may often appear in a Welsh guise as **Wrecsam**.

However, the problem can be more serious in other cases, as some places have very different names in Welsh and English. Where the inscription is written in Welsh it is likely that the Welsh form of the place name will appear. Here are some of the most important ones in different parts of Wales. In some areas there are very few English names. In others, like Pembrokeshire and the Vale of Glamorgan, even quite small villages have both an English name and a Welsh name, and the two are quite distinct.

North and central Wales

Aberhonddu	*Brecon*
Abermaw	*Barmouth*
Afon Menai, Y Fenai	*Menai Strait*
Caergybi	*Holyhead*
Dinbych	*Denbigh*
Y Drenewydd	*Newtown*
Y Felinheli	*Port Dinorwic*
Llanelwy	*St Asaph*
Llanfair ym Muallt	*Builth*
Porthaethwy	*Menai Bridge*
Y Trallwm,Y Trallwng	*Welshpool*
Trefaldwyn	*Montgomery*
Trefyclo	*Knighton*
Y Waun	*Chirk*
Yr Wyddgrug	*Mold*
Ynys Enlli	*Bardsey island*

South-west Wales

Aberdaugleddau	*Milford Haven*
Abergwaun	*Fishguard*
Aberteifi	*Cardigan*
Caerfyrddin	*Carmarthen*
Castell Newydd Emlyn	*Newcastle Emlyn*
Dinbych y Pysgod	*Tenby*
Hendy Gwyn ar Daf	*Whitland*
Hwlfordd	*Haverfordwest*
Llanbedr Pont Steffan	*Lampeter*
Llandudoch	*St Dogmael's*
Penfro	*Pembroke*

Talacharn	*Laugharne*
Trefdraeth	*Newport (Pembs)*
Tyddewi	*St David's*

Smaller villages in Pembrokeshire

Casblaidd	*Wolf's Castle*
Casfuwch	*Castle Bythe*
Casmael	*Puncheston*
Casnewydd Bach	*Little Newcastle*
Castell Henri	*Henry's Moat*
Y Garn	*Roch*
Nanhyfer, Nyfer	*Nevern*
Treamlod	*Ambleston*
Treletert	*Letterston*
Tremarchog	*St Nicholas*
Trewyddel	*Moylegrove*

South-east Wales

Aberpennar	*Mountain Ash*
Abertawe	*Swansea*
Y Bontfaen	*Cowbridge*
Brynbuga	*Usk*
Caerdydd	*Cardiff*
Casgwent	*Chepstow*
Casnewydd	*Newport (Mon)*
Castell Nedd	*Neath*
Y Fenni	*Abergavenny*
Penybont ar Ogwr	*Bridgend*
Treforus	*Morriston*

Smaller villages in the Vale of Glamorgan

Llanbedr y Fro	*Peterston super Ely*
Llandudwg	*Tythegston*
Llanddunwyd	*Welsh St Donats*
Llanfihangel ar Elai	*Michaelston super Ely*
Llangrallo	*Coychurch*
Llanilltud Fawr	*Llantwit Major*
Llansanffraid	*St Bride's super Ely*
Trebefered	*Boverton*
Trefflemin	*Flemingston*
Tresimwn	*Bonvilston*

There are often references to the county in which a parish or village is located. Until modern changes to the local government system there were traditionally thirteen counties in Wales. These have very different names in Welsh and English, as shown below. The word **sir** (*county*) may appear before the name, or this may be omitted:

Aberteifi	Sir Aberteifi	*Cardiganshire*
Brycheiniog	Sir Frycheiniog	*Breconshire*
Caerfyrddin	Sir Gaerfyrddin	*Carmarthenshire*
Caernarfon	Sir Gaernarfon	*Carnarvonshire*
Dinbych	Sir Ddinbych	*Denbighshire*
Fflint	Sir y Fflint	*Flintshire*
Maesyfed	Sir Faesyfed	*Radnorshire*
Meirionnydd	Sir Feirionnydd	*Merionethshire*
Môn	Sir Fôn	*Anglesey*
Morgannwg	Sir Forgannwg	*Glamorganshire*
Mynwy	Sir Fynwy	*Monmouthshire*
Penfro	Sir Benfro	*Pembrokeshire*
Trefaldwyn	Sir Drefaldwyn	*Montgomeryshire*

Place-names outside Wales

Occasionally the place referred to is outside Wales. The person commemorated may have moved away and lived in England or further afield. Or it may be that he or she died elsewhere, lost at sea or in war. Place-names outside Wales are usually given in the normal English form, but not always: where there is a recognised Welsh equivalent to the English name, this does sometimes appear:

Countries

Yr Aifft, Yr Aipht	*Egypt*
Yr Almaen	*Germany*
Yr Eidal	*Italy*
Ffrainc	*France*
Iwerddon	*Ireland*
Lloegr	*England*
Palesteina	*Palestine*

Seas

Môr Iwerydd	*Atlantic*
Y Môr Tawel	*Pacific*
Môr y Canoldir	*Mediterranean*

Towns and cities

Bryste	*Bristol*
Caer	*Chester*
Caergaint	*Canterbury*
Caergrawnt	*Cambridge*
Lerpwl	*Liverpool*
Llundain	*London*
Llynlleifiad	*Liverpool*

Manceinion	*Manchester*
Rhydychen	*Oxford*

More general terms for *north, south, east* and *west* are also used in this context:

gogledd	*north*
de	*south*
gorllewin	*west*
dwyrain	*east*
Gogledd America	*(the) North (of) America*
Dwyrain Affrica	*(the) East (of) Africa*

Formerly of ...

One further complication is that the person commemorated may not have been living locally at the time of death, but may have had a previous local connection:

genedigol o	*by birth from*
gynt o	*formerly from*
diweddar o	*formerly from*
genedigol o'r plwyf hwn	*by birth from this parish*
gynt o blwyf Llannon	*formerly from (the) parish (of) Llannon*
diweddar o Hendre yn y plwyf hwn	*formerly from Hendre in this parish*

Now try these:

See if you can translate the wording shown in these photographs, using the phrases explained in this section. (Answers on page 63.)

1.

2.

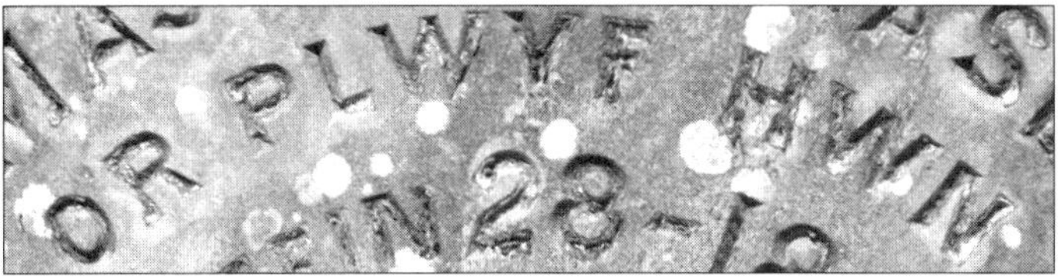

3.

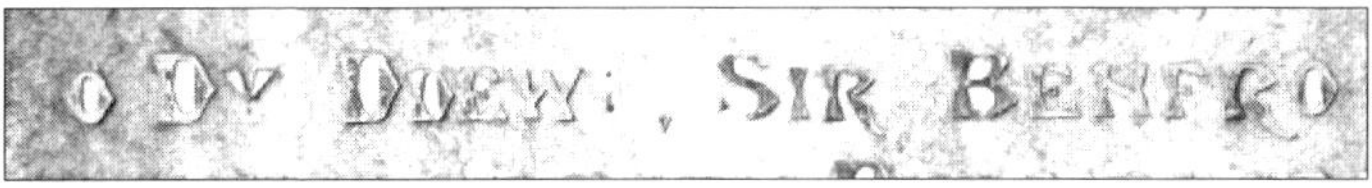

4.

Answers: 1: *from this place*; 2: *from this parish*; 3: *from St David's, Pembrokeshire*; 4:*Swansea*

Incomers: where did they come from?

As the industrial revolution changed the face of south east Wales in the nineteenth century, Cardiff grew steadily to meet the increasing demand for its services as a port. People from England, Scotland, Ireland and, of course, all parts of Wales came here to make a new life. The inscriptions on their gravestones often reveal their origins, and there is no difficulty when the places referred to are in English – Birmingham, Dewsbury, Honiton Clyst, Inverness. If the wording is in Welsh, however, you may need to look more closely to work out where they came from.

Place-names such as Aberystwyth, which are written in the same way in both languages, are straightforward, though even then it can be puzzling when the place-name appears embedded in a more complicated phrase. We see that Mair Williams, who died in 1902 aged sixty-three, was **gynt o dref Aberystwyth**. What is going on here? A careful check on the wording shows that this merely says *formerly of the town of Aberystwyth*. No real problem.

Other inscriptions contain place names which are not so straightforward. Mary Jenkins, who died in 1844 aged twenty-nine, is described as **genedigol gerllaw Llanbedr Pont Steffan**. Something of a challenge, but again one which can be sorted out quite easily. First the place-name. **Llanbedr Pont Steffan** is just the Welsh name for Lampeter in west Wales, and looking up the other words here reveals that she was **genedigol** (*by birth*) from somewhere **gerllaw** (*near*) there. Being able to interpret such comments as this can be of great help in tracing the history of the family. It would be clear now that Mary had not lived very long in Cardiff, and that the next step would be to look for records in the Lampeter area.

The two inscriptions quoted here are from gravestones in the Heath Cemetery, but this is not the only early one in Cardiff. You might want to check also the old cemetery in Adamsdown which preceded it, and there are of course also many churchyards and chapel burial grounds in the city and in the former villages, now suburbs, which surround it.

6

'Who died ...'

There are many different ways of saying that someone has died, in Welsh as in English, varying from the simple and straightforward to phrases giving greater detail about the circumstances.

Simple phrases

The Welsh word corresponding to *to die* is **marw**, which appears in various set phrases.

bu farw	*died (of a man or a woman)*
a fu farw	*who died*
yr hwn a fu farw	*who died (of a man)*
yr hon a fu farw	*who died (of a woman)*
buont feirw	*died (of several people)*
y rhai a fuont feirw	*who died (of several people)*

Where the inscription records the death of several people from the same family, usually children who died young, the phrase **fel y canlyn** *(as follows)* often appears before a list of names and dates.

buont feirw fel y canlyn	*died (of several people) as follows*
y rhai a fuont feirw fel y canlyn	*who died (of several people) as follows*

In other inscriptions the plain form **bu farw** *(died)* is replaced by a phrase with a more religious tone.

hunodd	*fell asleep*
hunodd yn yr Iesu	*fell asleep in Jesus*
hunodd yn yr Arglwydd	*fell asleep in the Lord*
hunasant yn yr Arglwydd	*fell asleep in the Lord (of several people)*
gorffennodd ei yrfa ddaearol	*finished his earthly life*
gorffennodd ei gyrfa ddaearol	*finished her earthly life*
gorffwysodd oddi wrth ei lafur	*rested from his labour*
gorffwysodd oddi wrth ei llafur	*rested from her labour*
aeth adref	*went home*
cymerwyd adref	*was taken home*
galwyd i fywyd helaethach	*was called to a more abundant life*
galwyd oddiwrth ei waith at ei wobr	*was called from his work to his reward*
galwyd oddiwrth ei gwaith at ei gwobr	*was called from her work to her reward*
ymadawodd â'r fuchedd hon	*departed from this life*
ymadawodd â'r bywyd hwn	*departed from this life*
ymadawodd â'r byd hwn	*departed from this world*
ymadawsant â'r bywyd hwn	*departed from this life (of several people)*

There can be a further elaboration, describing the troubled or transient life that has been left behind:

diflanedig	*transient*
helbulus	*troubled*
presennol	*present*
terfysglyd	*troubled*
trallodus	*sorrowful*
ymadawodd â'r byd helbulus hwn	*departed from this troubled life*
ymadawodd â'r fuchedd bresennol hon	*departed from this present life*

And where a religious formula such as one of these is used, there may also be a phrase containing the word **gobaith** *(hope)*, looking ahead to something better:

mewn gobaith am fywyd gwell	*in hope of (a) better life*
tan obaith o adgyfodiad llawen	*in hope of (a) joyful resurrection*

Circumstances

Occasionally a phrase will be added to make it clear that the death recorded was sudden and unexpected, or on the other hand quiet and peaceful:

annisgwyl	*unexpected*
disymwth	*sudden*
disyfyd	*sudden*
sydyn	*sudden*

yn annisgwyl	*unexpectedly*
yn ddisymwth	*suddenly*
yn ddisyfyd	*suddenly*
yn sydyn	*suddenly*
mewn hedd	*in peace*
tawel	*quiet*
yn dawel	*quietly*

Or other phrases may be added to elaborate on the circumstances. Death may have occurred as the result of an accident or illness, or a woman may have died in childbirth. Look out for the following words:

damwain	*accident*
damwain angheuol	*fatal accident*
cystudd	*illness*
nychdod	*lingering illness*
salwch	*illness*
geni, genedigaeth	*birth*
ysbyty	*hospital*
blin	*grievous*
byr	*short*
hir	*long*
maith	*long*
trwm	*heavy*
trwy ddamwain	*through (an) accident*
ar ôl cystudd byr	*after (a) short illness*
ar ôl hir nychdod	*after (a) long illness*

ar ôl salwch hir	*after (a) long illness*
ar eni ei phlentyn	*at (the) birth (of) her child*

Where the death was the result of an accident or disaster, we often find other more specific forms instead of the general **bu farw** (*died*):

collodd ei fywyd	*lost his life*
collodd ei bywyd	*lost her life*
collwyd	*was lost*
cafodd ei ddiwedd	*had his end*
cafodd ei diwedd	*had her end*
cyfarfu â'i ddiwedd	*met his end*
cyfarfu â'i diwedd	*met her end*
cafodd ei ladd	*was killed (of a man)*
cafodd ei lladd	*was killed (of a woman)*
lladdwyd	*was killed*
boddodd	*drowned*
bu foddi	*drowned*
boddwyd	*was drowned*

Other phrases appear in the context of death in war:

cwympodd	*fell*
syrthiodd	*fell*
rhoddodd ei fywyd	*gave his life*
aberthodd ei fywyd	*sacrificed his life*

It is clearly not possible to list all the various situations which might arise, but it is worth looking out for certain key phrases, used in commonly-occurring circumstances:

Colliery/quarry/railway disaster

tanchwa	*explosion*
ffrwydriad	*explosion*
glofa	*colliery*
yng nglofa X	*in X colliery*
gwaith	*works*
pwll glo	*colliery*
ym mhwll glo X	*in X colliery*
chwarel	*quarry*
yn chwarel X	*in X quarry*
rheilffordd	*railway*

Lost at sea

ar y môr	*at sea*
ar fwrdd	*on board*
agerlong	*steamship*
llestr	*vessel (ship)*
llong	*ship*
mordaith rhwng X a Y	*(a) voyage between X and Y*
mordaith o X i Y	*(a) voyage from X to Y*
ar fordaith	*on (a) voyage*
ar ei fordaith	*on his voyage*
drylliad	*wreck*
llongddrylliad	*shipwreck*
suddiad	*sinking*
storm	*storm*

Died in war

aberth	*sacrifice*
dros ei wlad	*for his country*
ar faes y frwydr	*on the battlefield*
ar faes y gad	*on the battlefield*
mewn brwydr	*in (a) battle*
trwy law y gelyn	*at (the) hand (of) the enemy*
yn y rhyfel mawr	*in the great war*
yn y ffosydd	*in the trenches*
clwyfwyd	*was wounded*
o'i glwyfau	*from his wounds*
mynwent filwrol	*military cemetery*

And was buried

Some inscriptions go into greater detail, noting not only when the death occurred and what the circumstances were, but also when the actual burial took place. Dates are given for both events. (Chapter 7 explains how to read dates such as those given here.)

a hunodd 24 Hydref 1842	*who died 24 October 1842*
ac a gladdwyd 29 Hydref 1842	*and who was buried 29 October 1842*

It will usually be clear that the person concerned is buried here, in this grave, and this may even be stated explicitly:

a fu farw yn ei gartref	*who died in his home*
ac a gladdwyd yma	*and who was buried here*

From time to time, however, the situation is more complicated, and you will find a person commemorated on a gravestone who is not actually buried there. This may be implicit, as for instance where the inscription mentions a death at sea. In other cases there may be detailed information about where the death occurred, and where the burial took place:

a fu farw yn Harlech ac a gladdwyd yno	*who died in Harlech* *and was buried there.*
a fu farw yng nghartref ei ferch ac a gladdwyd yn Llandeilo	*who died in (the) home (of)* *his daughter and was* *buried in Llandeilo*
a syrthiodd yn y rhyfel mawr ac a gladdwyd ym mynwent filwrol Ypres	*who fell in the great war* *and who was buried in (the)* *military cemetery (of)* *Ypres*

A number of different terms are used to refer to a cemetery in such phrases:

claddfa	*burial ground*
erw Duw	*(the) acre (of) God*
mynwent	*cemetery*

Occasionally there is no reference to the actual death as such, only to the burial, and the date given appears to be that of the burial.

Cremation became fully legal in 1902, though there are records of some cremations earlier than this. Occasionally an inscription will refer to a cremation:

corfflosgiad	*cremation*
llwch	*ashes*

corfflosgiad ym Mhontypridd	*cremation in Pontypridd*
claddwyd ei lwch yn Aberdâr	*his ashes were buried in Aberdare*
claddwyd ei llwch yn Aberdâr	*her ashes were buried in Aberdare*

Now try these:

See if you can translate the wording shown in these photographs, using the phrases explained in this section. (Answers on page 75.)

1.

2.

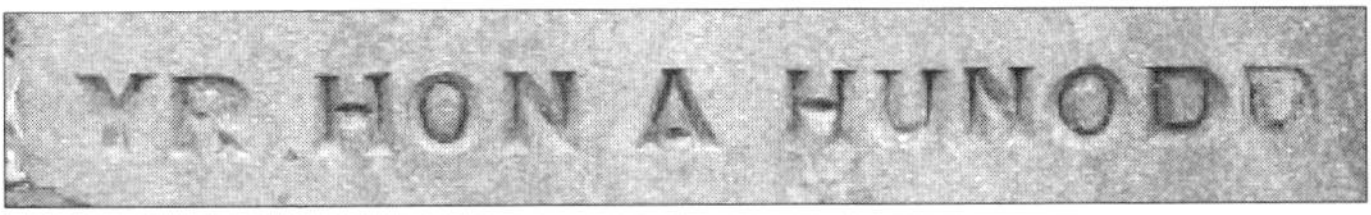

3.

4.

Answers: *1: died; 2: who (a woman) fell asleep; 3: who (a woman) departed from this life; 4: who died through (an) accident in Tylwydyn colliery*

Sudden death

Work in a mine, a quarry or on the railway brought its own dangers, and many men met an untimely death in an accident or an explosion. One of these was William Owen, who died aged only twenty-eight in 1864. His grave can be seen in the burial ground of Bethesda Chapel, near Narberth, and the inscription records starkly: **Bu farw trwy anffawd yn Narberth Rd Station** *(He died through an accident at Narberth Rd Station).* No further details appear, and we would have to search elsewhere for the full story. There is, however, also a poem which stresses how sudden and unexpected was his death.

Ar forau gwaith yr aethum ma's,
Heb ganfod cledd yr angau glas,
Cyn dod yn ol ce's farwol glwy';
A phawb o'r bron rwy'n madel mwy.

One morning I set out,
Not seeing the sword of pale death,
Before coming back I received a mortal wound;
Now I take my leave of everyone.

This poem appears across a wide area in south and west Wales. Sometimes, as here, we know that death was the result of an accident. Elsewhere there is nothing to say what happened, and the poem is the only indication of sudden death. It is striking, however, that those commemorated in this way are often either quite young or at least in the prime of life: between four years old, and fifty-one. To me this suggests that the death was not a natural one and that it would be worth asking more questions about the circumstances.

Poems such as this are also interesting for the light they shed on the way the Welsh language has developed over the years. The word **ma's** *(out)* at the end of the first line is very much a feature of south Wales dialect, and the fact that it is so crucial to the rhyme suggests that we are dealing here with a poem which comes from the south, and reflects southern speech. The northern equivalent **allan** *(out)* would not work at all here. The phrase **angau glas** *(pale death – lit. death pale)* is revealing too. In the modern language **glas** corresponds to *blue*, but in the old days it had a much wider remit, including *green*, *blue*, *grey* and *pale*. This commemorative poem has preserved the old usage, and we find examples right up to the early twentieth century.

7

Dates

Most inscriptions give the date when the person commemorated died, and the usual format for this is as shown below. The day is given as a number, which may come before or after the month, and then the year is given last:

3 Ionawr, 1843	*3 January, 1843*
Ebrill 15, 1895	*April 15, 1895*
9 Chwef, 1901	*9 Feb, 1901*

The name of the month may be given in full or, if this name is rather long, it may appear in an abbreviated form, to save space.

Ionawr	Ion.	*January*
Chwefror	Chwef.	*February*
Mawrth	Maw.	*March*
Ebrill	Ebr.	*April*
Mai		*May*
Mehefin	Meh.	*June*
Gorffennaf, Gorphenhaf	Gorff., Gorph.	*July*
Awst		*August*
Medi		*September*
Hydref	Hyd.	*October*
Tachwedd	Tach.	*November*
Rhagfyr	Rhag.	*December*

An alternative format is for the date to be given in the form corresponding to *first*, *second* and so on, with a short sequence of letters, corresponding to *1st*, *2nd* in English. These follow the actual number, and should not cause any difficulty, as they always appear alongside this number:

3ydd Ionawr, 1843	*3rd January, 1843*
Ebrill 15fed, 1895	*April 15th, 1895*
9fed Chwef, 1901	*9th Feb, 1901*

It is possible, though unusual, for the date to be given in words rather than numbers, but for completeness these forms are given below, together with the corresponding abbreviations, which may appear following numbers as above:

cyntaf	1af	*first*
ail	2il	*second*
trydydd	3ydd	*third*
pedwerydd	4ydd	*fourth*
pumed	5ed	*fifth*
chweched	6ed	*sixth*
seithfed	7fed	*seventh*
wythfed	8fed	*eighth*
nawfed	9fed	*ninth*
degfed	10fed	*tenth*
unfed ar ddeg	11eg	*eleventh*
deuddegfed	12fed	*twelfth*
trydydd ar ddeg	13eg	*thirteenth*
pedwerydd ar ddeg	14eg	*fourteenth*
pymthegfed	15fed	*fifteenth*
unfed ar bymtheg	16eg	*sixteenth*
ail ar bymtheg	17eg	*seventeenth*

deunawfed	18fed	*eighteenth*
pedwerydd ar bymtheg	19eg	*nineteenth*
ugeinfed	20fed	*twentieth*
unfed ar hugain	21ain	*twenty-first*
ail ar hugain	22ain	*twenty-second*
trydydd ar hugain	23ain	*twenty-third*
pedwerydd ar hugain	24ain	*twenty-fourth*
pumed ar hugain	25ain	*twenty-fifth*
chweched ar hugain	26ain	*twenty-sixth*
seithfed ar hugain	27ain	*twenty-seventh*
wythfed ar hugain	28ain	*twenty-eighth*
nawfed ar hugain	29ain	*twenty-ninth*
degfed ar hugain	30ain	*thirtieth*
unfed ar ddeg ar hugain	31ain	*thirty-first*

Sometimes this format may be expanded to give fuller forms, using words such as *day, month* and *year*:

dydd	*day*
mis	*month*
blwyddyn	*year*
y 7fed dydd o fis Mai yn y flwyddyn 1834	*the 7th day of (the) month (of) May* *in the year 1834*
y 3ydd o fis Ionawr yn y flwyddyn 1843	*the 3rd of (the) month (of) January* *in the year 1843*

Occasionally there is reference to a death having occurred at the time of one of the main religious festivals, *Christmas*, for instance, or *Easter*, or at some other noteworthy time of the year:

Y Nadolig	*Christmas*
Y Pasg	*Easter*
Gwener y Groglith	*Good Friday*
Sul y Pasg	*Easter Sunday*
Y Sulgwyn	*Whitsun*
Dydd Calan	*New Year's Day*

Or the actual day of the week may be mentioned:

Dydd Sul	*Sunday*
Dydd Llun	*Monday*
Dydd Mawrth	*Tuesday*
Dydd Mercher	*Wednesday*
Dydd Iau	*Thursday*
Dydd Gwener	*Friday*
Dydd Sadwrn	*Saturday*

If the person commemorated died in the morning, a modified form using the word **bore** (*morning*) may be used:

bore	*morning*
fore Sul	*(on) (the) morning (of) Sunday*

Now try these:

See if you can translate the wording shown in these photographs, using the phrases explained in this section. (Answers on page 82.)

1.

2.

3.

4.

Answers: 1: *March 22nd 1871;* 2: *February 12, 1927;* 3: *Wednesday June 23, 1909;* 4: *Dec. 28. 1861*

Death in Childbirth

Many women died in childbirth, or shortly afterwards, from complications or fevers which could not be treated in those days. This seems to have been accepted as normal, and many inscriptions do not spell out the details in full. It is only when we read the poem that we see what really happened.

Mary Morris from Henllan Amgoed, for instance, died in 1844 aged thirty. The baby died too, and both are buried together.

Mi gollais i fy mywyd brau,
Wrth ddwyn un bach i'r byd:
Hunwn yma ni ein dau,
Y bedd yw ein cartref gyd.

I lost my fragile life,
Bringing a little one into the world:
We both sleep here
The grave is our home.

Mary Jones from Plwmp died in 1861 aged twenty, and here, too, the baby also died:

Yn ysgafn sengwch gylch y fan,
Lle'r hunaf fi a'm baban gwan,
Mewn tawel gwsg 'nol diwedd taith,
O'r byd i drag'wyddoldeb maith.

Tread lightly around the place,
Where I and my weak baby sleep,
In a quiet sleep after the end of the journey,
From the world to long eternity.

We are forced to recognise how different life was in the past, how our expectations and assumptions have changed over the years.

There is not always a poem to tell the story, however, or there may be a poem but it is too general in its message to be of any help. This where it may be important to look carefully at the dates on the gravestone. I remember seeing an inscription in Dinas, north Pembrokeshire, which recorded the death of a young woman, Margaret Rowland, who died on May 27th 1849 aged twenty-seven. Later the inscription notes, without comment, that her son John died on May 19th 1849 aged 7 days. It is only when we look again more closely at these dates that we realise what must have happened. John was born on May 12th and died a week later on the 19th. Margaret, the mother, lived on for another week, and died herself on the 27th. The story is all there, but we need to put the facts together ourselves to make sense of it.

8

Age at death

Inscriptions usually indicate too how old the person commemorated was when he or she died, and this may be expressed in a number of different ways.

Adults and Children

Some phrases are used for both adults and children. The actual age is given as a number, and the word **blwydd** (*year*) may be included or left out, or indeed appear as an abbreviation. Note that the form used for *year* in Welsh when discussing ages is slightly different from the form used in discussing dates, as seen above:

oed, oedran	*age*
blwyddyn	*year (dates)*
blwydd	*year (ages)*
yn 6 oed	*aged 6*
yn 2 oed	*aged 2*
yn 25 oed	*aged 25*
yn 6 blwydd oed	*aged 6 years*
yn 2 flwydd oed	*aged 2 years*
yn 25 mlwydd oed	*aged 25 years*
yn 6 bl. oed	*aged 6 yrs.*
yn 2 fl. oed	*aged 2 yrs.*
yn 25 ml. oed	*aged 25 yrs.*

Another set of phrases are also used very generally, but they will vary a little in form according to whether the deceased was a man or a woman:

ei oed 43 mlwydd	*his age 43 years*
ei hoed 43 mlwydd	*her age 43 years*
yn 43 o'i oedran	*aged 43 (of a man)*
yn 43 o'i hoedran	*aged 43 (of a woman)*
yn y 44 flwyddyn o'i oedran	*in the 44 year of his age*
yn y 44 flwyddyn o'i hoedran	*in the 44 year of her age*

Children

One of the saddest aspects of this work is realising the number of children who died very young from what would today be mild childhood illnesses, and the distress of the parents can be seen in their determination to record the exact age at which the child died. We find not just **blwydd** (*year*) here, but a range of other words too.

diwrnod	*day*
wythnos	*week*
pythefnos	*fortnight*
mis	*month*
blwydd	*year*

These may appear singly, or in varying combinations:

yn wythnos oed	*aged a week*	*one week old*
yn bythefnos oed	*aged a fortnight*	*a fortnight old*
yn fis oed	*aged a month*	*one month old*
yn flwydd oed	*aged a year*	*one year old*

yn 3 diwrnod oed	*aged 3 days*	*3 days old*
yn 7 wythnos oed	*aged 7 weeks*	*7 weeks old*
yn 6 blwydd, 5 mis a 5 diwrnod oed	*aged 6 years, 5 months and 5 days*	*6 years, 5 months and 5 days old*

Occasionally, instead of giving the exact age of the child, the inscription will look ahead to the age not yet attained:

cyn cyrraedd	*before reaching*
cyn cyrraedd blwydd oed	*before reaching a year old*
cyn cyrraedd 6 blwydd oed	*before reaching 6 years old*

Numbers expressed in words

It is normal for the age of the person commemorated to be given in figures, as above, but occasionally this will be spelled out in words. The numbers up to 10 were given earlier in Chapter 4, and can be used here too:

yn chwe blwydd oed	*aged six years*
yn ddeg mlwydd oed	*aged ten years*
yn chwech oed	*aged six*
yn ddeg oed	*aged ten*

As was pointed out then, some numbers have a different form when referring to men and to women; **dau** is used for men or boys, but **dwy** for women or girls. The word **blwydd** (*year*) is grammatically feminine in Welsh, and will always take the female form of the number, regardless of the sex of the person commemorated. Even if the word **blwydd** (*year*) is left out, the female form of the number will still appear.

yn ddwy flwydd oed	*aged two years*
yn ddwy oed	*aged two*

Once you go beyond ten, the traditional number system in Welsh is very complex, and very different to the decimal system normal in English. Look out for the following words, which will be an indication that what you have is indeed a phrase specifying age:

deuddeg	*twelve*	
pymtheg	*fifteen*	*lit. five-ten*
deunaw	*eighteen*	*lit. two-nine*
ugain	*twenty*	
deugain	*forty*	*lit. two-twenty*
hanner cant	*fifty*	*lit. half (a) hundred*
trigain	*sixty*	*lit. three-twenty*
pedwar ugain	*eighty*	*lit. four-twenty*

yn bymtheg mlwydd oed	*aged fifteen years*
yn ugain mlwydd oed	*aged twenty years*
yn hanner cant oed	*aged fifty*
yn bedwar ugain oed	*aged eighty*

Other numbers are built up using these as a basis, as in the examples below. It's helpful, perhaps, to think of the rather old-fashioned English numbers 'five-and-twenty' (for 'twenty-five'), and to remember the Biblical 'three score years and ten', which is the old way of saying 'seventy years'. The system is complex and it is not realistic to give all possible ages here. If you come across a form such as this which appears to indicate age, then you will need to ask a native speaker for help in working out the exact age of the person commemorated in the inscription:

yn un ar bymtheg oed	*aged sixteen*	*lit. one on fifteen*
yn bump ar hugain oed	*aged twenty five*	*lit. five on twenty*
yn naw a thrigain oed	*aged sixty-nine*	*lit. nine and sixty*
yn un ar bymtheg a deugain	*aged fifty-six*	*lit. one on fifteen and forty*

General indications of age

At other times the inscription is much less detailed, giving only a general indication of age. This is often found where a child has died in infancy:

yn ei fabandod	*in infancy (of a boy)*
yn ei babandod	*in infancy (of a girl)*
yn eu babandod/mabandod	*in infancy (of several children)*

Similar phrases used with reference to adults are shown below:

yn fam ifanc	*as a young mother*
ym mlodau ei ddyddiau	*in his prime*
ym mlodau ei dyddiau	*in her prime*
mewn henaint teg	*in a good old age*

Alternative format

Sometimes the age of the person commemorated is not spelled out as such, but rather the date when he or she was born is given and then the date when he or she died. There are several phrases corresponding to *born*. Chapter 6 gave the most common ones for *died*:

ganwyd	*was born*
ganed	*was born*
cafodd ei eni	*was born (of a man)*
cafodd ei geni	*was born (of a woman)*

Here are some examples of this format in use:

ganwyd 3ydd Medi, 1842	*was born 3rd September, 1842*
bu farw 16eg Rhagfyr, 1897	*died 16th December, 1897*
ganed 24 Chwefror, 1875	*was born 24 February, 1875*
hunodd 2 Mehefin, 1910	*fell asleep 2 June, 1910*

It is possible, of course, to work out the age of the deceased from this information, even though it is not spelt out directly.

Now try these:

See if you can translate the wording shown in these photographs, using the phrases explained in this section. (Answers on page 91.)

1.

2.

3.

4.

Answers: *1: aged (a) week; 2: aged 65; 3: aged 51 years; 4:aged 2 years and 4 months*

Other Languages

Throughout this handbook the focus is on Welsh-language inscriptions, and how to read them. We should, however, bear in mind that there are other possibilities. An inscription which is clearly not English, may well be Welsh – indeed it probably is – but we do find other languages too. The simplest situation is where a pious thought in Latin has been added. It would have been assumed at one time that all educated people could read Latin, and would have no difficulty with this. In the churchyard at Llandough near Cowbridge, for instance, we find just such a Latin couplet on the grave of Elias Basset who died in 1726.

In Brachiis Saluatoris mei
Vivere volo, et mori cupio.

In the arms of my Saviour
I wish to live, and hope to die.

Other languages may be more significant when it comes to family history. Did a member of the family come from another country to settle here? If so, then some at least of the wording on early gravestones may appear in the home language, and you may need help to work out what they say.

In the churchyard at Llantrisant, for instance, there is a memorial to Bridget Egan Roberts. The first part of the inscription is in English and the basic facts are clear. She was born near Portumna in county Galway in 1835, came to Wales to live, and died here in 1891. At least some of the family were Welsh-speaking, as there is also a Welsh poem in the inscription. What is really interesting, howevcr, is the phrase which appears between the English facts and the Welsh poem, without any explanation.

Oraid ar anmain Brigde, ingine Fenburra Ui Madagain.

Pray for the soul of Brigid, the daughter of Finbar O'Madagain.

When I first saw this, it seemed likely that the phrase must be in Irish, given the rest of the inscription, but I could not be sure. I had to go and find an Irish-speaker who could translate it for me, and confirm that what I had suspected was true. In itself this was interesting, and suggested that she also spoke Irish. From the point of view of family history, however, what is really important is that some of the core information about Bridget Egan Roberts is only available in the Irish phrase. Having succeeded in reading this, we now now who her father was, and that her maiden name must have been O'Madagain. As a result we have a reasonable chance of following up her family back in Ireland, something which would have been difficult otherwise.

Inscriptions such as this are not particularly common, but it could just be that you come up against one as you follow up the family's history. It would be well worth the extra work of finding out which language you are dealing with, and what the inscription actually says.

9

Social status

In many inscriptions there is some further indication of the social status of the person commemorated. This may be in terms of a profession or craft, involvement in cultural activities, or as a member of the church or chapel.

Status in the world of work

Many different types of working life are recorded in these inscriptions. The terms we find may relate to work in education or medicine, public service or local or central government. The deceased may have practised a craft or run a business, or may have been a farmer or a sailor. Sometimes, alongside the term denoting the work carried out, or even instead of it, there will be a word like **ysgol** (*school)* or **siop** (*shop*) which has clear implications as to social status:

Education

athro	*teacher (of a man)*
athrawes	*teacher (of a woman)*
coleg	*college*
cyfarwyddwr addysg	*director of education*
darlithydd	*lecturer*
myfyriwr	*student*
prifathro	*headmaster*
prifathrawes	*headmistress*
prifysgol	*university*
ysgolfeistr	*teacher (of a man)*

ysgolfeistres	*teacher (of a woman)*
ysgol	*school*

Medicine

bydwraig	*midwife*
deintydd	*dentist*
fferyllydd	*pharmacist*
meddyg	*doctor*
metron	*matron*
milfeddyg	*vet, farrier*
nyrs	*nurse*
physigwr	*physician*

Public service

arolygydd	*supervisor, superintendent*
clerc	*clerk*
cyfreithiwr	*lawyer*
gorsaf-feistr	*station master*
heddgeidwad	*policeman*
heddlu	*police force*
meistres elusendy	*mistress (of) almshouse*
meistres tloty	*mistress (of) poorhouse*
milwr	*soldier*
swyddog	*officer*

Local or central government

aelod	*member*
Aelod Seneddol, AS	*Member of Parliament, MP*
cyngor	*council*
cynghorydd	*councillor*

henadur	*alderman*
maer	*mayor*
sirydd	*sheriff*
Ynad Heddwch, YH	*Justice of the Peace, JP*

Craft

adeiladydd	*builder*
argraffydd	*printer*
asiedydd	*joiner*
crefftwr	*craftsman*
crwynwr	*tanner*
crydd	*shoemaker*
gof	*smith*
gwehydd	*weaver*
gwniadwraig	*dressmaker*
melinydd	*miller*
peiriannydd	*engineer*
plastrwr	*plasterer*
saer, saer coed	*carpenter*
saer llongau	*shipwright*
saer maen	*mason*

Business

arwydd	*sign (as outside a public house)*
cariwr	*carrier*
dilledydd	*draper*
llyfrwerthwr	*bookseller*
masnachwr	*merchant*
masnachydd	*merchant*
siop	*shop*

Farming

amaethwr	*farmer*
bugail	*shepherd*
deilad	*tenant*
ffarmwr	*farmer*
garddwr	*gardener*

Seamen

cadben	*captain (of a ship)*
llong	*ship*
llongwr	*sailor*
llywydd	*captain (of a ship)*
morwr	*sailor*
peilot	*pilot (of a ship)*

Mining and quarrying

chwarelwr	*quarryman*
glöwr	*coalminer*
mwynwr	*miner*

General service

gwas	*servant*
gweithiwr	*worker*

Surprisingly the term which refers to a profession is sometimes in English, even in a Welsh-language inscription. For instance a form such *Master Mariner* will commonly be found even though the rest of the wording is in Welsh. It is possible that people were accustomed to using such technical expressions of status in

English, and had no straightforward Welsh equivalent term to hand.

Occasionally it will be specified that the person commemorated had formerly carried out a particular profession, and this is shown by adding **cyn** (*former*) to the word concerned. Or it will be specified that he or she was in a senior post, by adding **prif** (*chief*) to the relevant word:

cyn-athro	*former teacher*
prif beiriannydd	*chief engineer*

Cultural status

In other cases the information provided refers not to the professional status of the person commemorated, but rather to his or her position as a well-known poet, writer or patriot:

arloeswr	*pioneer*
bardd	*poet*
cerddor	*musician*
cymwynaswr	*benefactor*
emynydd	*hymn writer*
geiriadurwr	*writer of dictionaries*
golygydd	*editor*
gwirfoddolwr	*volunteer*
gwladgarwr	*patriot*
hynafieithydd	*antiquarian*
llenor	*writer*
telynor	*harpist (of a man)*
telynores	*harpist (of a woman)*

Many Welsh poets have published their work under a name which differs in some way from their normal, everyday name.

This is not a serious attempt to disguise their identity, but rather a way of distinguishing their role as a poet from their role in the everyday world as a teacher, preacher or bank worker. The poet **Eliseus Williams**, for instance, worked as a clerk and accountant for the North Wales Slate Company, but published his poetry and was widely known throughout Wales as **Eifion Wyn**. An inscription commemorating a poet, even a comparatively local and little known one, will often give his bardic name in brackets, after his real one:

> John Morgan (Ioan Trithyd)
> Griffith Jones (Gutyn Prysor)
> Ebenezer Thomas (Eben Fardd)

The bardic name will often, as here, include two elements. The first is usually a variant on the poet's first name - **Ioan** for **John**, **Gutyn** for **Griffith, Eben** for **Ebenezer**. The second may be an indication of where the poet came from - **Trithyd** for the village of **Llantrithyd, Prysor** for **Cwm Prysor**. Or it may be simply the word **bardd** (*poet*). Musicians and singers, too, may be referred to in this way, with their stage name given alongside their real name.

A little care is needed here, as there is also a tendency in more recent times to give not only the correct name of the person commemorated in the inscription, but also a nickname in brackets, if this was widely used by family and friends. It is usually clear, however, which of these tendencies is involved in any one case:

> Florence Morgan (Flossie)
> John Evan Jones (Jack)

Status in religion

Nonconformists and Anglicans use rather different terminology in referring to the rôles played by an individual in the organisation of the church or chapel. The range of rôles in a Nonconformist chapel will include the following:

Nonconformists

aelod	*member*
arolygwr yr Ysgol Sul	*supervisor (of) the Sunday School*
arolygwr yr Ysgol Sabothol	*supervisor (of) the Sunday School*
athro/athrawes yn yr Ysgol Sul	*teacher in the Sunday School*
athro/athrawes yn yr Ysgol Sabothol	*teacher in the Sunday School*
arweinydd y canu	*leader of singing*
arweinydd y gân	*leader of song*
blaenor	*deacon*
bugail	*shepherd (= minister)*
cenhadwr	*missonary*
codwr canu	*leader of singing*
diacon	*deacon*
dirwestwr	*abstainer from alcohol*
diwygiwr	*revivalist*
gweinidog (yr efengyl)	*minister (of the gospel)*
pregethwr	*preacher*
sefydlydd, sefydlwyr	*founder, founders*
sylfaenydd, sylfaenwyr	*founder, founders*
trysorydd	*treasurer*
ysgrifennydd	*secretary*

Alternatively there may be a reference to the work carried out, without the use of a formal title. Look out for phrases such as these:

bu yn glanhau	*cleaned (ie. the chapel)*
bu yn gofalu am	*cared for*
bu yn gwasanaethu	*served*
bu yn gweinidogaethu	*ministered*
bu yn pregethu	*preached*

Nonconformists will usually mention at some point the actual denomination involved:

Annibynwyr	*Independents*
Bedyddwyr	*Baptists*
Crynwyr	*Quakers*
Cymdeithas y Cyfeillion	*Society of Friends (Quakers)*
Methodistiaid	*Methodists*
Methodistiaid Calfinaidd	*Calvinistic Methodists*
Methodistiaid Wesleaidd	*Wesleyan Methodists*
Presbyteriaid	*Presbyterians*
Trefnyddion Calfinaidd	*Calvinistic Methodists*
Trefnyddion Wesleyaidd	*Wesleyan Methodists*
Undodwyr	*Unitarians*
Wesleyaid	*Wesleyans*

But there is also use of more general terminology which does not make direct reference to the denomination:

capel	*chapel*	
cysegr	*sanctuary*	*ie. church or chapel*
eglwys	*church*	
tŷ cwrdd	*chapel*	*lit. meeting house*

achos	*cause*	*ie. church or chapel*
gwinllan	*vineyard*	*ie. church or chapel*

Anglican roles, and consequently terminology, are rather different:

Anglicans

clochydd	*sexton*
curad	*curate*
ficer	*vicar*
goruchwyliwr	*overseer*
offeiriad	*priest*
periglor	*priest*
prebendwr	*prebendiary*
rheithor	*rector*
warden	*churchwarden*

Note that the title **Parchedig** or **Parch**. is used for both Nonconformist minsters and Anglican clergy:

Y Parchedig John Hughes	*The Reverend John Hughes*
Y Parch. John Hughes	*The Rev. John Hughes*

And other more general terminology is of course common ground.

yr Arglwydd	*the Lord*
Gwaredwr	*Redeemer*
Prynwr	*Redeemer*
yr Iesu	*Jesus*
Iesu Grist	*Jesus Christ*

Both traditions praise faithfulness and hard work, using words such as those shown below to do so.

cyfrifol	*responsible*
cymeradwy	*worthy*
da	*good*
defnyddiol	*useful*
diwyd	*diligent*
doeth	*wise*
ffyddlon	*faithful*
gweithgar	*hardworking*
gwerthfawr	*valuable*
llafurus	*hardworking*
parchus	*respected*
ymdrechgar	*hard working*
ymroddedig	*devoted*

And both traditions will note how long a particular role was held. This may be done in very general terms.

dros amryw o flynyddoedd	*for many years*
am nifer fawr o flynyddoedd	*for a great many years*
am lawer o flynyddoedd	*for many years*

It is more usual, however, to spell out exactly how many years of service were given, using numbers and either **blynedd** (*year*) or **blynyddoedd** (*years*). Note that the form **blynedd** (*year*), used here in expressing periods of time, is different to the forms given earlier for discussing dates or ages.

blwyddyn	*year (dates)*
blwydd	*year (ages)*
blynedd	*year (length of time)*
blynyddoedd, blynyddau	*years*

am 20 mlynedd	*for 20 years*	*lit. for 20 year*
dros 25 mlynedd	*over 25 years*	*lit. over 25 year*
am 32 o flynyddoedd	*for 32 years*	*lit. for 32 of years*
dros 15 o flynyddoedd	*over 15 years*	*lit. over 15 of years*

The phrase may be further expanded, by the use of words which mean *a period of time*:

cyfnod	*period of time*
ysbaid	*period of time*
am ysbaid o 23 mlynedd	*for a period of 23 years*
am gyfnod o 19 o flynyddoedd	*for a period of 19 years*

The number of years is usually expressed with figures, as in the examples above. It may occasionally, however, be spelled out in words:

am ysbaid o ugain mlynedd	*for a period of twenty years*
am bump ar hugain o flynyddoedd	*for twenty five years*

If this happens, you will need to refer back to Chapter 4 for the numbers up to ten, and to Chapter 8 for the numbers above ten. As was mentioned earlier, the number system above ten is complex in Welsh, and you may need to consult a native speaker to establish exactly how long the period of service lasted.

Now try these:

See if you can translate the wording shown in these photographs, using the phrases explained in this section. (Answers on page 105.)

1.

2.

3.

4.

Answers: 1: *(a) deacon of this church*; 2: *The Rev. Wm. Jones*; 3: *(a) weaver*; 4: *J.P.*

Death at Sea

Villages along the coast of Wales looked to the sea for a livelihood. The men went to sea and travelled the world, the women stayed at home and looked after the smallholding and the children. Inevitably many men and boys were lost in storms or accidents, and the gravestones record the loss of a father or son at sea, alongside the names of those who died at home and were buried there. Dinas Cross in north Pembrokeshire is typical. Short accounts which can only hint at what really happened:

a fu farw pan ar fordaith o Newcastle i San Francisco

who died while on a voyage from Newcastle to San Francisco

a gollodd ei fywyd ar y môr, trwy foddi, trwy i agerdd-long redeg twy ei lestr ef

who lost his life at sea, by drowning, as a steam-ship ran through his vessel

An appropriate Biblical verse may appear, for instance: A rhoddodd y môr i fyny y meirw oedd ynddo (*And the sea gave up the dead which were in it*) (Revelation 20.13). Or there may be a poem, musing on the meaning of death at sea:

Bu farw ar y môr, –
Ond wele'r dyfrllyd fedd
A egyr ffordd y saint
I wlad tragwyddol hedd.

He died at sea, –
But behold the watery grave
Which opens the way of the saints
To the country of eternal peace.

Not every sailor, of course, was lost. Many came home safe and well and lived on to a good age, and the inscription will often include a poem contrasting the hard life at sea with a peaceful old age and burial on land:

Wedi hwylio wyneb moroedd,
Cwrdd a llawer o groeswyntoedd,
Braint cael cartref mwyn fy mhriod
A chael yn Machpelah feddrod.

After sailing the surface of the sea,
Meeting many crosswinds,
It is a privilege to have the loving home of my wife
And to have a grave in Machpelah.

This poem may in fact be a crucial source of information. The body of the inscription is often comparatively short, giving us little more than the date when the person commemorated died and how old he was. Only the poem tells us that he had been a seaman, and adds greatly to the picture we are able to form of his life and times.

10

Additional burials

An inscription often commemorates a number of different people, usually members of the same family. It will start by giving details of the first person commemorated, and is then extended as additional burials take place. These later additions on the whole follow the same conventions as have been set out already. There are two points to watch out for. Firstly, they are often linked to the existing inscription by specific words, corresponding to *also* in English.

hefyd	*also*
eto, etto	*again*
yr un modd	*in the same way*
ac, a	*and*

The inscription then procedes as usual, giving the expected details. The name of the person commemorated, when he or she died, and age at death.

The second point of interest is the way family relationships are expressed. The way this additional person was related to those already commemorated is often explicitly spelled out, using a set of very specific forms:

yr uchod	*the above*
y dywededig	*the said (of a man)*
y <u>ddywededig</u>	*the said (of a woman)*
yr enwedig	*the named*

y rhagddywededig	*the aforesaid*
y rhag-grybwylledig	*the above-mentioned*
a enwir uchod	*who is named above*
a enwyd uchod	*who was named above*
a grybwyllwyd uchod	*who was mentioned above*
yr hwn a enwyd uchod	*who was named above (of a man)*
yr hon a enwyd uchod	*who was named above (of a woman)*
y rhai a enwyd uchod	*who were named above (of several people)*

The person commemorated may be simply referred to as, for instance, *son of the above*, or *son to the above*, or the name of the original person may be added for completeness:

mab yr uchod	*(the) son (of) the above*
gweddw y rhagddywededig	*(the) widow (of) the aforesaid*
mab i'r uchod	*son to the above*
mab y James Davies uchod	*(the) son (of) the above James Davies*
gweddw y dywededig Owen Morgan	*(the) widow (of) the said Owen Morgan*
mab i'r John Evans uchod	*son to the above John Evans*

Another way of linking to the person already commemorated is less formal, and involves the use of words such as *his, her, their* to refer back. In the alternative format this option gives to him, *to her, to them:*

ei fab	*his son*
ei briod	*his spouse (= wife)*

ei phriod	*her spouse (= husband)*
eu mab	*their son*
tri o'i blant	*three of his children*
tri o'i phlant	*three of her children*
tri o'u plant	*three of their children*
mab iddo	*son to him*
wyres iddi	*grand-daughter to her*
plant iddynt	*children to them*

Where several children from the same family died in succession, the form **arall** (*other*) may also be used:

arall	*other (of one person)*
eraill	*other (of several people)*
ei ferch arall	*his other daughter*
merch arall iddo	*(an) other daughter to him*
eu plant eraill	*their other children*

Less usually the order in which people died may be indicated by the use of the words *preceded* and *followed:*

rhagflaenodd	*preceded*
dilynodd	*followed*
a ragflaenodd ei dad	*who preceded his father*
a ddilynodd ei mam	*who followed her mother*

This link with the person already commemorated can extend to the account of where they lived, and the time when they died:

o'r plwyf uchod	*from the above parish*
o'r lle uchod	*from the above place*

o'r un plwyf	*from the same parish*
o'r un lle	*from the same place*
yr un amser	*the same time*
yr un pryd	*the same time*

The inscription may even specify that they are all buried in the same grave, or indicate the location of adjacent burials:

yn yr un bedd	*in the same grave*
wrth ystlys	*by (the) side (of)*
ar y dde	*on the right*
ar y chwith	*on the left*
ar yr aswy	*on the left*
yr ochr ogleddol	*the northern side*
yr ochr ddeheuol	*the southern side*
yr ochr ddwyreiniol	*the eastern side*
yr ochr orllewinol	*the western side*

Now try these:

See if you can translate the wording shown in these photographs, using the phrases explained in this section. (Answers on page 112.)

1.

2.

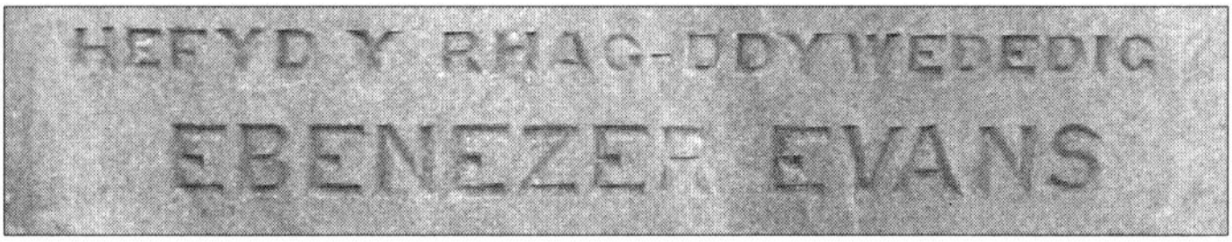

3.

4.

Answers: *1: also John their son; 2: also the above mentioned Ebenezer Evans; 3: also Mary (the) widow (of) the above; 4: who (a man) was named above*

Changing the Wording

Many inscriptions are used to commemorate more than one person. The original wording tells us about the first person to die, and then further details are added as other family members are buried in the same grave. The lettering is often different in these later additions to the inscription, making it clear that not all the wording was carved at the same time. There may even be a change of language, with the earlier sections in Welsh and the later ones in English.

Sometimes, however, the family go much further, as I discovered a few years ago in Llangefni churchyard. The gravestones had been moved and placed against the actual church wall, and I was looking for examples of a poem I was interested in at the time. Sure enough there it was:

Wrth fyned heibio cofia ddyn
Mae fel rwyt tithau finnau a fum
Ac fel rwyf finnau tithau a ddeui
Ystyria ddyn mae marw a wneu.

As you go by remember man
That as you are I was
And as I am you shall come
Consider man that you will die.

It appeared on the gravestone of one William Jones, who died in 1839 aged forty-three. So far nothing unusual. A few minutes later I noticed another example of the poem, this time with *we* rather than *I* in the second and third lines.

... Mae fel rwyt tithau ninau a fu'm
Ac fel yr um ninau tithau a ddeui ...

... That as you are we were
And as we are you shall come ...

I was not surprised to see a slightly different form of the poem, as such changes are quite common, but the reason for the change here was completely unexpected. Here once again was the name of William Jones who died in 1839 aged forty-three. But I've just seen his gravestone, I thought. What is going on here? This time, however, below his name was another, his daughter Grace Jones, who died in 1857 aged twenty-five. Two people now commemorated, not one, and an explanation for the change in wording.

Why did the family decide to have a new gravestone carved, with both names and a modified poem? Why didn't they just add the new name at the end of the inscription, in the usual way? We will probably never know.

11

Who erected the memorial?

There is usually no mention of who erected the gravestone, and the assumption is that the family was responsible. Sometimes, however, the inscription makes this clear, and names the members of the family who carried out this task. In other cases, where the person commemorated was an important member of the community, the memorial was erected by members of the chapel or some other group, and this information is given in the inscription.

The stone itself, and the act of erecting it, are usually referred to with one of the following phrases:

codwyd	*was raised*
cyfodwyd	*was raised*
gosodwyd	*was set up*
rhoddwyd	*was given*
dadorchuddiwyd	*was unveiled*
carreg	*stone*
colofn	*column*
cofadail	*memorial*
rhoddwyd y garreg hon	*this stone was given*
cyfodwyd y golofn hon	*this column was raised*
gosodwyd y gofadail hon	*this memorial was set up*

Those responsible are then named:

ei briod a'i blant	*his wife and his children*
eu plant	*their children*
edmygwyr	*admirers*
cyfeillion	*friends*
cydweithwyr	*fellow workers*
cymdeithas	*society*
undeb	*union*
gan ei blant	*by his children*
gan ei gyfeillion	*by his friends*
gan ei gydweithwyr	*by his fellow workers*
gan Gymdeithas y Gwyneddigion	*by (the) Society (of) Gwyneddigion*
gan Undeb yr Alcanwyr	*by (the) Union (of) Tinplate Workers*

A slightly different formula is found in some cases:

rhodd gan ei phlant	*(a) gift by her children*
rhodd gan ei gyfeillion	*(a) gift by his friends*
rhodd Ysgol Sul Bethania	*(the) gift (of) Bethania Sunday School*

Other phrases often found include the following.

parch	*respect*
teyrnged	*tribute*
fel arwydd o barch	*as (a) sign of respect*
yn deyrnged o barch	*as (a) tribute of respect*

There may also be a reference to the cost of the funeral and the memorial, and who paid for it.

angladd	*funeral*
claddedigaeth	*funeral*
cynhebrwng	*funeral*
talwyd	*were paid*
treuliau	*costs*
talwyd treuliau'r angladd	*(the) costs (of) the funeral were paid*
rhoddion	*subscription, gifts*
tanysgrifiadau	*subscription*
trwy roddion cyhoeddus	*by public subscription*
trwy danysgrifiadau cyhoeddus	*by public subscription*

And other additions are occasionally found which refer to the practicalities of setting up and caring for the memorial.

cerfiwyd gan	*carved by*
atgyweiriwyd gan	*repaired by*

Additions which are not confined to such public memorials, but appear from time to time on ordinary gravestones include references to this being the first burial in a new plot, and to the ownership of the grave and whether it may be opened again.

y cyntaf a gladdwyd yn y fynwent hon	*the first who was buried in this cemetery*
ni agorir y bedd hwn heb ganiatad ...	*this grave is not to be opened without (the) permission (of) ...*
nid yw'r bedd hwn i'w agor eto	*this grave is not to be opened again*

Now try these:

See if you can translate the wording shown in these photographs, using the phrases explained in this section. (Answers below.)

1.

2.

Answers: 1: *This memorial column is (the) fruit (of the) love (of) his admirers;* 2: *This column was raised through public donations*

Forgotten Heroes

Who was William Lewis? And why is there a substantial memorial gravestone commemorating him in Cwmbwrla, Swansea? Babell Chapel has been demolished, but the old burial ground is still there, and up at the far end, by the wall, is a fine granite obelisk with a book carved in marble, bearing the words *Tinman's Companion*, and an inscription in Welsh. We see that he died in 1887, aged forty-nine, but the name is not a familiar one. Nor is the other name by which he was known, Lewys Afan, also given here.

There are in fact three sets of clues here. First the carved book, already mentioned. Next a poem which refers to him as **y dewr alcanydd** (*the brave tinman*), who worked for **hawliau'i frodyr** (*his brothers' rights*), and calls him **y doeth gynllunydd** (*the wise organiser)*. At the end of the inscription we then find this dedication:

> Gosodwyd y gofgolofn hon gan Undeb yr /
> Alcanwyr fel arwydd o barch i'r ymadawedig.

> *This memorial was set up by the Union of /*
> *Tinplate Workers as a mark of respect to the departed.*

Clearly he was held in great respect, and it seems strange that he is not better known today. His name is not in the online Dictionary of Welsh Biography, and it proves quite hard to find out more.

In fact I found this memorial as a spin-off from my own family history research. My grandfather, Stan Awbery, was from Swansea, and throughout his life both an active worker in the Labour movement and a keen amateur historian. Back in 1949 he published an account of the early days, and here I found the story of William Lewis. He had founded the Union of Tinplate Workers in 1870, and spent his short life working to improve the conditions of workers in the industry. His book became known as the Tinplate Workers' Bible and was the basis for negotiations over pay. Hardly surprising that they contributed to the cost of erecting his memorial.

We all know of memorials to the great and the good. Maybe the work being carried out now by family historians will shed more light on forgotten heroes like William Lewis, people who made a real contribution to the community, but whose memory has over the years faded and been almost lost.

12

Biblical verses

The inscription may often also include a Biblical verse or a short poem, or indeed both. These can come either at the beginning, or after the main factual section, and are worth noting as they often shed further light on the circumstances and the feelings of the family.

They may, of course, appear in an inscription which is all in Welsh, but are also used in a rather different way. Even in a strongly Welsh-speaking area the main part of the inscription is often in English, with a Biblical verse or poem in Welsh following this. Clearly the people who chose the inscription could speak Welsh, so why use English here as well? What we have to remember is that the only language with official status in Wales for many years was English, and many people may well have felt that the formal record of the death should therefore be in English, the inscription on the gravestone being seen almost as a legal document. They seem then to have felt free to add a Biblical verse or poem in Welsh.

What is important from the point of view of family history is that this becomes the only indication that the family were Welsh-speaking at the time. This is, of course, particularly interesting if the family no longer speaks Welsh, and you are trying to establish at what point they changed to English.

Some of these Biblical verses are very popular, and widely used over a long period of time. They come from the traditional Welsh Bible, originally translated in 1588 by Bishop William Morgan, and used with only minor revisions till a modern translation was published in 1988. This is the equivalent in Welsh of the Authorised Version in English, though it actually predates the English by some forty years. Here are some of the more commonly found verses, together with the English equivalents. You will not always find the whole verse in the inscription. Sometimes there will be just a short phrase taken from the verse, perhaps because there is not enough space for the whole.

Dysg i ni felly gyfrif ein dyddiau, fel y dygom ein calon i ddoethineb.
So teach us to number our days, that we may apply our hearts to wisdom.

[Psalm 90.12]

Gwerthfawr yng ngolwg yr Arglwydd yw marwolaeth ei saint ef.
Precious in the sight of the Lord is the death of his saints.

[Psalm 116.15]

Nac ymffrostia o'r dydd yfory: canys ni wyddost beth a ddigwydd mewn diwrnod.
Boast not thyself of tomorrow; for thou knowest not what a day may bring forth.

[Proverbs 27.1]

Gwyliwch gan hynny: am na wyddoch pa awr y daw eich Arglwydd.
Watch therefore: for ye know not what hour your Lord doth come.

[Matthew 24.42]

Am hynny byddwch chwithau barod: canys yn yr awr ni thybioch y daw Mab y dyn.
Therefore be ye also ready: for in such an hour as ye think not the Son of man cometh.

[Matthew 24.44]

Canys byw i mi yw Crist a marw sydd elw.
For to me to live is Christ and to die is gain.

[Philippians 1.21]

Gwyn eu byd y meirw y rhai sydd yn marw yn yr Arglwydd.
Blessed are the dead which die in the Lord.

[Revelation 14.13]

Other verses are more specific, and can be taken to refer directly to the circumstances of the death commemorated in the inscription. Some are used where a child has died, and others where someone has died comparatively young, or in old age:

The Death of a Child

Yr Arglwydd a roddodd, a'r Arglwydd a ddygodd ymaith; bendigedig fyddo enw yr Arglwydd.
The Lord gave, and the Lord hath taken away; blessed be the name of the Lord.

[Job 1.21]

Fel blodeuyn y daw allan ac y torrir ef ymaith.
He cometh forth like a flower and is cut down.

[Job 14.2]

Gadewch i'r plant bychain ddyfod ataf fi, ac na waherddwch hwynt, canys eiddo'r cyfryw rai yw teyrnas Dduw.

Suffer little children to come unto me, and forbid them not: for of such is the kingdom of God.

[Luke 18.16]

(Also similar verses at Matthew 19.14 and Mark 10.14)

Death at a Comparatively Young Age

Gostyngodd efe fy nerth ar y ffordd; byrhaodd fy nyddiau.
He weakened my strength in the way; he shortened my days.

[Psalm 102.23]

Ei haul a fachludodd tra yr oedd hi yn ddydd.
His/her sun is gone down while it was yet day.

[Jeremiah 15.9]

Death in Old Age

Ti a ddeui mewn henaint i'r bedd fel y cyfyd ysgafn o yd yn ei amser.
Thou shallt come to thy grave in a full age, like as a shock of corn cometh in his season.

[Job 5.26]

Digonaf ef â hir ddyddiau, a dangosaf iddo fy iachawdwriaeth.
With long life will I satisfy him, and shew him my salvation.

[Psalm 91.16]

Others again can be seen as a comment on the character of the person commemorated, praising their character or piety:

Praise of the Departed

Coffadwriaeth y cyfiawn sydd fendigedig.
The memory of the just is blessed.

[Proverbs 10.7]

Hyn a allodd hon, hi a'i gwnaeth.
She hath done what she could.

[Mark 14.8]

Mi a ymdrechais ymdrech deg, mi a orphenais fy ngyrfa, mi a gedwais y ffydd.
I have fought the good fight, I have finished my course, I have kept the faith.

[II Timothy 4.7]

There is in fact a tendency to adapt some of these verses which praise the character of the departed, so that they fit the family circumstances better. For instance the original form of Mark 14.8, shown above, is worded as praise of a woman, but can also appear – reworded – so as to express praise of a man. The original form of another verse shown above, II Timothy 4.7, is worded as praise of one person, but also appears – reworded – so as to praise more than one person, usually a husband and wife commemorated together:

Modified Verses

Hyn a allodd hwn, efe a'i gwnaeth.
He hath done what he could.

[Mark 14.8]

Ni a ymdrechasom ymdrech deg, ni a orphenasom ein gyrfa, ni a gadwasom y ffydd.
We have fought the good fight, we have finished our course, we have kept the faith.

[II Timothy 4.7.]

Normally there is no indication of why a particular verse was chosen for the inscription, but occasionally there may be a comment that this was the deceased's favourite verse, or even that these were his or her last words:

adnod	*Biblical verse*
geiriau	*words*
ei hoff adnod	*his / her favourite verse*
ei eiriau olaf	*his last words*
ei geiriau olaf	*her last words*

The books of the Bible

Often the verse appears alone, with no indication of where it appears in the Bible. There seems to have been an assumption that the reader would be sufficiently familiar with the Welsh Bible for this not to be necessary. Occasionally, however, it will be followed by an abbreviation which indicates the book from which it is taken, and then also the chapter and verse. Some books of the Bible have identical names in Welsh and English – *Ruth, Samuel, Esther, Job, Daniel, Amos*. Others may appear unfamiliar because they are spelled differently in Welsh, *Jeremiah* in English but **Jeremeia** in Welsh. And there are some whose names are very different in the two languages, *Proverbs* in English but **Diarhebion** in Welsh. Here are the Welsh names of those books which are most likely to cause difficulties if you come across them, together with the abbreviation normally used:

Old Testament

Barnwyr	Barn.	*Judges*
Brenhinoedd	Bren.	*Kings*
Cronicl	Cron.	*Chronicles*

Salmau	Salm.	*Psalms*
Diarhebion	Diar.	*Proverbs*
Pregethwr	Preg.	*Ecclesiastes*
Eseia	Es.	*Isaiah*
Sephaneia	Seph.	*Zephaniah*
Sechareia	Sech.	*Zechariah*

New Testament

Sant Mathew	Math.	*Matthew*
Sant Marc	Marc	*Mark*
Sant Luc	Luc	*Luke*
Sant Ioan	Ioan	*John*
Rhufeiniaid	Rhuf.	*Romans*
Corinthiaid	Cor.	*Corinthians*
Philipiaid	Phil.	*Philippians*
Thesaloniaid	Thes.	*Thessalonians*
Timotheus	Tim.	*Timothy*
Hebreaid	Heb.	*Hebrews*
Iago	Iag.	*James*
Datguddiad	Dat.	*Revelation*

Pious Thoughts

Some phrases look like Biblical verses but are not. They may come from the wording of the traditional funeral service:

> Ynghanol ein bywyd yr ydym yn angau
> *In the midst of life we are in death.*

Or they may be short phrases, regularly used in this context but not quotations from any particular source.

Atgofion melys	*Sweet memories*
Byth mewn cof	*Ever in memory*
Hedd, Heddwch	*Peace*
Hedd Perffaith Hedd	*Peace Perfect Peace*
Gorffwys mewn Hedd	*Rest in Peace*
Gyda'i gilydd	*Together*
Melys yw'r atgofion	*Sweet are the memories*
Tangnefedd	*Peace*
Wedi'r gwaith gorffwys	*After work rest*
Ynghyd	*Together*

Now try these:

See if you can translate the wording shown in these photographs, using the phrases explained in this section. (Answers on page 129.)

1.

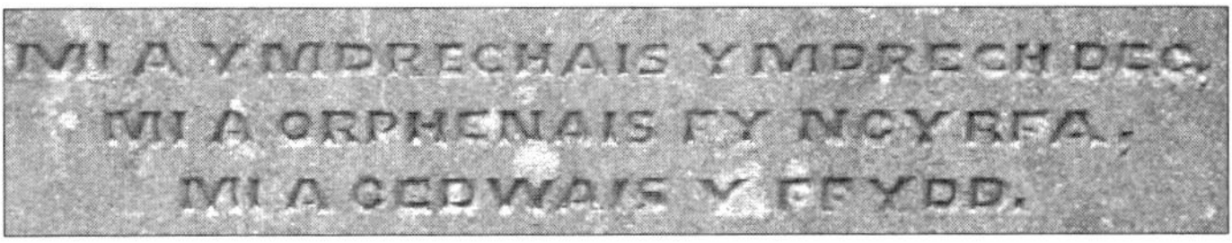

MI A YMDRECHAIS YMDRECH DEG,
MI A ORPHENAIS FY NGYRFA,
MI A GEDWAIS Y FFYDD.

2.

"TI A DDEUI MEWN HENAINT I'R BEDD,
FEL Y CYFYD YSGAFN O ŶD YN EI
AMSER" JOB V. 26.

3.

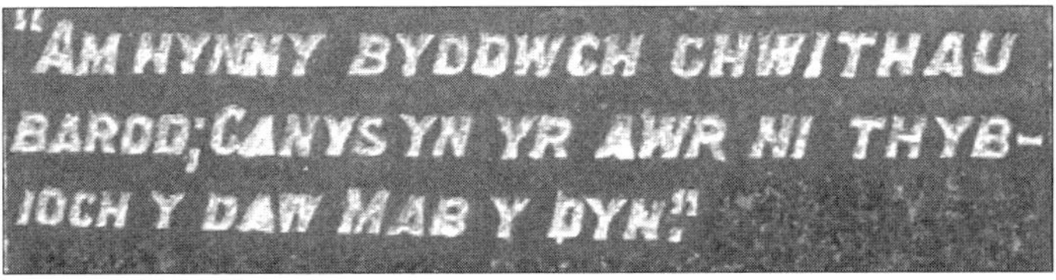

"AM HYNNY BYDDWCH CHWITHAU
BAROD; CANYS YN YR AWR NI THYB-
IOCH Y DAW MAB Y DYN."

4.

Answers: *1: I have fought the good fight, I have finished my course, I have kept the faith (see p.125); 2: Thou shalt come to thy grave in a full age, like as a shock of corn cometh in his season (see p.124); 3: Therefore be ye also ready, for in such an hour as ye think not the Son of man cometh (see p.123); 4: Peace, Perfect Peace (see p.128)*

Changing Attitudes

Many Welsh gravestones have a Biblical verse, or more than one, as part of the inscription. This is so common a pattern that we may take it for granted, and pay little attention to these verses, assuming that they are not really relevant to our interests. This may indeed be the case if family history only concerns establishing the specific detail of names, dates and relationships. If we take a broader view, however, and wish to see how the family's experiences and attitudes fit into the social context in which they lived, there may be useful material here.

Over the years it appears that changes have occurred in how Biblical verses have been chosen, and how they have been used. In the nineteenth century they are used in a straightforwardly religious manner, with a stress on the brevity of life, the unpredictability of death. Verses such as these are common:

> Dyn a aned o wraig sydd fyr o ddyddiau, a llawn o helbul.
> *Man that is born of a woman is of few days, and full of trouble.* *Job 14.1*

> Nac ymffrostia o'r dydd yfory: canys ni wyddost beth a ddigwydd mewn diwrnod.
> *Boast not thyself of tomorrow; for thou knowest not what a day may bring forth.*
> Proverbs 27.1

A family using such a verse is clearly part of the wider religious community, church or chapel, echoing traditional themes. As we move into the twentieth century, however, the way these verses are used seems to change. More and more often they are used, not to express religious truths, but rather to praise the person commemorated. These are still Biblical verses, but the motivation for including them is different. We find such verses as these:

> Coffadwriaeth y cyfiawn sydd fendigedig.
> *The memory of the just is blessed.*
>
> Proverbs 10.7

> Mi a ymdrechais ymdrech deg, mi a orphenais fy ngyrfa, mi a gedwais y ffydd.
> *I have fought the good fight, I have finished my course, I have kept the faith.*
>
> II Timothy 4.7

The inscription is no longer a means of expressing religious faith, but rather a way for the family to record their memories of the person buried here.

This is the pattern of choice I have found in the Ely valley, to the west of Cardiff. Clearly we need to see if the same thing happens elsewhere, and to ask if the evidence from our own family gravestones is consistent with this change, or suggests a different way forward.

13

Poems

There is also a strong tradition of including a poem as part of an inscription. Here again it is common to find that the main part of the inscription is in English, but that it is followed by a Welsh poem. This poem is then the only indication that the family were at this stage Welsh-speaking.

Some of these poems are well-known, and appear in many inscriptions. Others are more personal, composed specifically to commemorate the individual buried here. If there is a poem in the inscription you are working on, then this again tells you something of the culture and attitudes of the family the time when it was included. It is impossible to list here all the possible poems you may find. The following discussion will give you some idea of the possibilities, but if you do find a poem and are interested in finding out more about it, you will need to find a Welsh-speaker with an interest in literature and ask for help.

Poems which turn up regularly are often the work of a well-known poet, and the poet's name may be shown in the inscription – though it may equally well be left out. When the name does appear, you may find either the poet's real name, here **Evan Evans**, or the "bardic name" which would have been used for literary purposes, here **Ieuan Glan Geirionnydd**:

> Mor ddedwydd yw y rhai trwy ffydd,
> Sy'n myn'd o blith y byw,
> Eu henwau'n perarogli sydd,
> A'u hun, mor dawel yw.
>
> Evan Evans [Ieuan Glan Geirionnydd]

How happy are those who through faith
Go from the midst of the living
Their names scent sweetly
And their sleep is so peaceful.

There is a tendency, as with Biblical verses, not to include the whole poem. In this case, for instance, you will often find only the last two lines, or the last line on its own. And again, as with Biblical verses, there is a tendency to adapt the wording to fit the circumstances. This poem was originally written in very general terms, referring to all those who have died in the faith. It can equally well appear, reworded, to refer to one person:

Modified Wording

Ei enw'n perarogli sydd
A'i hun, mor dawel yw.

His name scents sweetly
And his sleep is so peaceful.

Not all the poems which appear in inscriptions, however, are the work of a specific named poet. Many form part of a general folk tradition, and are widely used but of unknown origin. They appear across Wales, varying slightly in form from one example to another, but clearly conveying the same message. Here are two, one very general, the other found commemorating young children:

Cofia ddyn wrth fyned heibio,
Fel rwyt tithau finnau fuo,
Fel rwyf finnau tithau ddeui,
Cofia ddyn mai marw fyddi.

Remember man while going by
As you are so I was
As I am you shall come
Remember man that you will die.

Ni ddaeth y teg flodeuyn hyn
A ga'dd mor syn ei symud,
Ond i arddangos pa mor hardd
Yw blodau gardd y bywyd.

This lovely flower did not come
Which has been taken so suddenly
But to show how beautiful
Are the flowers of the garden of life.

The englyn

Most of these poems are short, probably so that they will fit into the space available on the gravestone, but there is one particular type widely used for inscriptions and worth watching out for. This is known as an **englyn**, and consists of four lines with strict rules relating to the length of each line, the rhyme scheme and patterns of alliteration within each line:

Iôr a biau roi bywyd – ac anadl,
Cu einioes ac iechyd;
Hawl a fedd i alw o fyd
Man y mynno mewn munud.
William Edwards [Wil Ysgeifiog]

The Lord owns the gift of life – and breath
Dear life and health
He has the right to call from the world
Where he choses in a moment.

Look for the distinctive layout. A long first line, with probably a dash – towards the end of the line; the word before the dash rhymes with the end of the following lines; one of the rhymes a short one-syllabled word, the others longer words. The second line is usually indented, and the third and fourth are indented but not so far. Many of these, like the one shown above, are famous poems and are found in many inscriptions across Wales. This one contains a general meditation on the fragility of life. Others look ahead to the Day of Judgement, or offer comfort to the parents of a child who has died:

Yr Iôr, pan ddelo'r ennyd, – ar ddiwedd,
    O'r ddaear a'n cyfyd;
  Bydd dorau beddau y byd
  Ar un gair yn agoryd.
Robert Williams [Robert ap Gwilym Ddu]

The Lord, when the time comes – at the end
Will raise us from the ground;
The doors of the graves of the world
At one word will open.

Trallodau beiau bywyd – ni welais
    Na wylwch o'm plegyd,
  Wyf iach o bob afiechyd
  Ac yn fy medd, gwyn fy myd.
Edward Richard

The sorrows and faults of life – I did not see
Do not weep for me,
I am well of all sickness
In my grave, blessed am I.

More interesting perhaps, in the context of family history, is that many of the poems found on gravestones have been specially written to commemorate a specific person. It is worth looking for instance to see if you can see a name in the poem, as in the example below. This could well be a hint that the poem was specially written for this individual. It is not a totally reliable indication, as the name could equally well have been added to an existing poem, to customise this as it were to the needs of the family. But this in itself would throw interesting light on the way the inscription has been devised and the willingness of the family to use and adapt the resources available to them:

Aeth Elen at ei theulu – a rhinwedd
Ar ei henw'n tyfu,
Hyd ael y bedd dal y bu
Drwy oes o blaid yr Iesu.

Elen went to her family – and virtue
Grows on her name
To the edge of the grave she continued
Through her life to serve Jesus.

As with Biblical verses, there is not usually any indication of why a particular poem has been chosen for the inscription. Occasionally it will be claimed that this was the deceased's favourite verse, or favourite hymn.

pennill	*verse (of a poem)*
emyn	*hymn*
ei hoff bennill	*his/her favourite verse*
ei hoff emyn	*his/her favourite hymn*

As this implies, the poem which appears is sometimes a well-known hymn, like the example below. Hymns are, however, by no means the only poems found on Welsh gravestones, and in fact are much less common than one might expect:

Arglwydd, arwain trwy'r anialwch
    Fi, bererin gwael ei wedd,
Nad oes ynof nerth na bywyd,
    Fel yn gorwedd yn y bedd:
        Hollalluog
    Ydyw'r un a'm cwyd i'r lan.
            William Williams [Pantycelyn]

Lord, lead through the desert
    Me, a poor pilgrim,
Who has no strength or life in me,
    As it were I lay in the grave:
        Almighty
    Is the one who carries me to the shore.

Now try these:

See if you can translate the wording shown in these photographs, using the phrases explained in this section. (Answers on page 138.)

1.

2.

3.

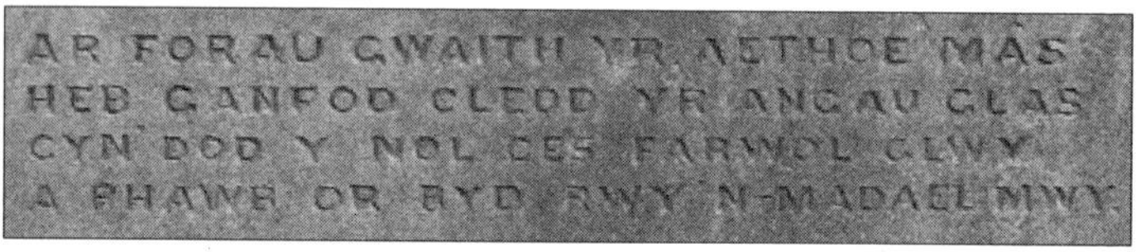

Answers: 1: *The Lord when the time comes – at the end / Will raise us from the ground; / The doors of the graves of the world / At one word will open.* (see p.135) 2: *How happy are those who through faith / Go from the midst of the living / Their names scent sweetly / And their sleep is so peaceful.* (see p.133) 3: *One morning I set out / Not seeing the sword of pale death / Before coming back I received a mortal wound / Now I take my leave of everyone.* (see p.76)

Local Poets

In Welsh tradition a poet was expected to serve the community, to produce a suitable verse whenever this was needed, celebrating a neighbour's good fortune or sharing in sadness and sorrow. People would often turn to the local poet for a verse to put on the gravestone when a member of the family died. Instead of drawing on the vast range of popular verses which are found right across the country, they often wanted something more personal, a poem which was unique and reflected their feeling of loss.

I found a very clear example of this in Castleton, a village on the old main road between Cardiff and Newport. The Welsh language has been in decline in this area for many years, but many of the gravestones in the burial ground of Salem, formerly the Baptist chapel, are in Welsh or partially in Welsh. Seven of the inscriptions contained a poem, above the name 'Gwrwst'. Here is one, commemorating Daniel Williams, who died in 1838 aged only seventeen:

Gwelwch drigfa mab gwiwlan - fwriwyd
Yn foreu ir marian
Ond Duw nef a'i lef yn lan
A digoll a'i dwg allan
Gwrwst

See the abode of a pure son - laid
Early in the ground
But the God of Heaven with his cry
Will raise him out pure and perfect.

Not great literature perhaps, but a competent and appropriate verse, reflecting the sadness of losing a son so young.

But who was Gwrwst, and why is his work on so many of the inscriptions in this burial ground? I had never seen this name anywhere else, so he must have been a local man. After much enquiry the mystery was resolved. It turns out that 'Gwrwst' was the name used, when writing poetry, by the Rev. Evan Jones, who was the minister of Salem from 1823 till his death in 1855. Of course Daniel and Mary William turned to him for a verse to put on the gravestone when their young son died, someone who had known the boy well and understood their grief. Of course he would have wanted to help in this way, and use his skills in traditional poetry to support members of his congregation.

14

What about mutated forms?

You may have a problem from time to time when trying to use the word list in the next section. If you were trying to check the meaning of **blant** or **mhlant** or **phlant**, for instance, you will have hit something of a brick wall. This section will help you to deal with this situation, where a Mutation Rule has changed the first letter of a word.

The mutation rules

The first letter of a word may change in one of three ways, and these are summarised in the table below. The first column shows which letters are affected, and the following three columns show how they may change. A word beginning with the letter **p**, such as **plant** (*children*), may end up as **blant** or **mhlant** or **phlant** depending on various features of the sentence where it has appeared. Mutations which are marked * in the table, are not considered standard Welsh, and may not be included in ordinary grammars of the language. They are, however, found in regional dialect and often appear in the inscriptions on gravestones.

Basic form	Soft Mutation	Nasal Mutation	Aspirate Mutation
p	b	mh	ph
t	d	nh	th
c	g	ngh	ch
b	f	m	
d	dd	n	
g	drop the 'g'	ng	
m	f		mh*
ll	l		
rh	r		
Vowel			add 'h'
n			nh*

Here are examples of these changes in action:

Basic Form	*but may also appear as*			
plant	blant	mhlant	phlant	*children*
tad	dad	nhad	thad	*father*
cof	gof	nghof	chof	*memory*
brawd	frawd	mrawd		*brother*
dinas	ddinas	ninas		*city*
glofa	lofa	nglofa		*coalmine*
merch	ferch		mherch*	*daughter*
llong	long			*ship*
rhan	ran			*part*
oed			hoed	*aged*
nain			nhain*	*grandmother*

Backtracking to the basic form

Having established what these changes are, we must now return to the practical problem. How do you decide whether what you have found in the inscription is the basic form, or has changed as a result of a Mutation Rule?

The first step is to look in the word list under the appropriate letter. If you are lucky, the word will be there, and you can check its meaning. What you found in the inscription was the basic form. No problem.

If the word is not there in the list, then you need a procedure to work out what its basic form is, so that you can check it out in the word list, and find the meaning. What follows below is a sort of reverse guide to the Mutation Rules. The outline which was given above has been turned on its head. First you see the mutated form, as it would appear in the inscription, and then the basic form which will appear in the word list. Using this guide should allow you to track back to the basic form in each case.

First Letter of Mutated Form		*First Letter of Basic Form*		
b	blant	**p**	plant	*children*
ch	chof	**c**	cof	*memory*
d	dad	**t**	tad	*father*
dd	ddinas	**d**	dinas	*city*
f	{frawd	**b**	brawd	*brother*
	{ferch	**m**	merch	*daughter*
g	gof	**c**	cof	*memory*
h	hoed	no **h**	oed	*aged*
l	long	**ll**	llong	*ship*
m	mrawd	**b**	brawd	*brother*
mh	{mhlant	**p**	plant	*children*
	{mherch	**m**	merch	*daughter*
n	ninas	**d**	dinas	*city*
ng	nglofa	**g**	glofa	*coal mine*
ngh	nghof	**c**	cof	*memory*
nh	{nhad	**t**	tad	*father*
	{nhain	**n**	nain	*grandmother*
ph	phlant	**p**	plant	*children*
r	ran	**rh**	rhan	*part*
th	thad	**t**	tad	*father*
--	lofa	**g**	glofa	*coal mine*

You will notice that some of the mutated letters in the first column correspond to more than one basic form. If the word starts with **nh** for instance, it may either backtrack to **t** or to **n**. The form **nhad** backtracks to **tad** (*father*), but **nhain** backtracks to **nain** (*grandmother*). In such situations you will have to try both options, until you find the form which appears in the word list.

One other set of examples is even more difficult to pin down, though not impossible. The table of mutation changes above showed that if the first letter of a word is **g**, then it may sometimes be dropped, so that **glofa** (*coalmine*) shows up as **lofa**. Backtracking here is more awkward, as the **g** could have been dropped from a wide variety of forms. The best approach is to look and see if the word you are checking is in the word list. If it is not, then try adding a **g** at the beginning, and have another look. This may well be the answer. Here are some more examples where adding a **g** takes you back to the basic form of the word:

First Letter of Mutated Form		*First Letter of Basic Form*	
anwyd	**g**	ganwyd	was born
eneth		geneth	girl, daughter
ogleddol		gogleddol	northern
weddw		gweddw	widow
wraig		gwraig	wife
yrfa		gyrfa	life

Place-names

Most of the mutations outlined here also affect place-names, and here are examples of the changes in action:

Basic Form	*but may also appear as*		
Pontypridd	Bontypridd	Mhontypridd	Phontypridd
Trefor	Drefor	Nhrefor	Threfor
Caerfyrddin	Gaerfyrddin	Nghaerfyrddin	Chaerfyrddin

Bangor	Fangor	Mangor
Dolgellau	Ddolgellau	Nolgellau
Gwersyllt	Wersyllt	Ngwersyllt
Machynlleth	Fachynlleth	
Llangollen	Langollen	
Rhydyfro	Rydyfro	

Here too, for completeness, is the reverse guide to mutations in place-names:

First Letter of Mutated Form		*First Letter of Basic Form*	
b	Bontypridd	**p**	Pontypridd
ch	Chaerfyrddin	**c**	Caerfyrddin
d	Drefor	**t**	Trefor
dd	Ddolgellau	**d**	Dolgellau
f	{Fangor	**b**	Bangor
	{Fachynlleth	**m**	Machynlleth
g	Gaerfyrddin	**c**	Caerfyrddin
l	Langollen	**ll**	Llangollen
m	Mangor	**b**	Bangor
mh	Mhontypridd	**p**	Pontypridd
n	Nolgellau	**d**	Dolgellau
ng	Ngwersyllt	**g**	Gwersyllt
ngh	Nghaerfyrddin	**c**	Caerfyrddin
nh	Nhrefor	**t**	Trefor
ph	Phontypridd	**p**	Pontypridd
r	Rydyfro	**rh**	Rhydyfro
th	Threfor	**t**	Trefor
--	Wersyllt	**g**	Gwersyllt

The same points should be borne in mind here as with ordinary words. In some cases the mutated letter in the first column corresponds to more than one basic form, and you will need to try out both to find the right answer. **Fangor** backtracks to **Bangor**, but **Fachynlleth** backtracks to **Machynlleth**.

In other cases you may need to try adding a **g** at the beginning to see if this gives you a likely place name:

First Letter of Mutated Form		*First Letter of Basic Form*
Lanllyn	**g**	Glanllyn
Lynebwy		Glynebwy
Wespyr		Gwespyr

Ambiguous forms

Occasionally you may find a pair of words which could be confused, though in fact all that is needed to resolve the problem is a look at the meaning of the phrase where the problematic word appears.

Take two words – **cof** (*memory*) and **gof** (*smith*) – both of which can appear on gravestones. The basic forms are different; **cof** begins with **c**, and **gof** begins with **g**. Normally there is no problem:

er cof am	*in memory of*
gof y pentref	*(the) smith (of) the village*

Unfortunately in certain situations a Mutation Rule will change **c** to **g**, so that the two words look the same:

er serchus gof am	in loving memory of
gof y pentref	(the) smith (of) the village

If this happens, then you will need to think about what would make sense in the phrase. Yes, the word **gof** appears in the word list as *smith*, but this does not make sense in the phrase **er serchus gof am**. Try again, and see if **gof** could possibly backtrack to something which does make sense, and of course it does, giving **cof** (*memory*).

Examples of this kind are rare, but it is worth bearing in mind that this might solve an apparent problem from time to time.

15

Word list

The following list includes all the various words you have met in the earlier sections of this handbook. This time they are given in normal alphabetic order, so that you can check up on items you find as you work on an inscription.

Where there is more than one recognised spelling for a word, these are all given. Inevitably, however, you will come across a range of other spellings from time to time which reflect local patterns of speech, and these cannot all be given here. One useful trick if you cannot find the word you are looking for, is to try substituting the letters **i, u** and **y** for each other. If for instance you find **blwiddin**, keep at it until you hit on **blwyddyn** (*year*), which is in the list. Or if you find **hefud**, in the same way try substituting till you find **hefyd** (*also*).

If you can't find the word you are looking for under the appropriate letter of the alphabet, try the previous chapter **What about Mutated Forms?** This will give you a set of procedures for backtracking from the mutated form, where the first letter has been changed, to the basic form. You will then be able to find this in the word list. If you are still unable to find a word, then it may be that the inscription you are reading contains unusual phrases, and you may need to consult a general Welsh-English dictionary.

Two sets of abbreviations are used here in specifying the meaning of words. Some forms are used only to refer to a man, and are marked *(m)*; others are only used to refer to a woman, and are marked *(f)*. Some forms refer to one person, and are marked *(sg)*; others refer to several people, and are marked *(pl)*.

a	*and*
a	*who*
Abergwaun	*Fishguard*
Aberhonddu	*Brecon*
Abermo	*Barmouth*
Aberpennar	*Mountain Ash*
Abertawe	*Swansea*
Aberteifi	*Cardigan, Cardiganshire, Ceredigion*
aberth	*sacrifice*
aberthodd	*sacrificed (sg)*
aberthu	*to sacrifice*
ac	*and*
achos	*cause*
addfwyn	*tender*
adeiladydd	*builder*
adgof, atgof	*remembrance*
adgyfodiad, atgyfodiad	*resurrection*
adnod	*Biblical verse*
adref	*towards home*
aelod	*member*
Aelod Seneddol, AS	*Member of Parliament, MP*
aeth	*went (sg)*
Afon Menai	*Menai Strait*
agerlong	*steamship*
agor	*to open*
agorir	*will be opened*
yr Aifft, yr Aipht	*Egypt*
ail	*second*
ail ar bymtheg	*seventeenth*
ail ar hugain	*twenty second*
yr Almaen	*Germany*
am	*of (in memory of)*
amaethwr	*farmer*
amryw	*many*
amser	*time*
angau	*death*
angheuol	*fatal*
angladd	*funeral*
angof	*forgetfulness*
Annibynwyr	*Independents*
annisgwyl	*unexpected*

annwyl, anwyl	*dear, beloved*
anwylaf	*dearest, most beloved*
anrhydeddus	*honourable*
ar	*on*
arall	*other (sg)*
ar fwrdd	*on board*
Arglwydd	*Lord*
argraffydd	*printer*
arloeswr	*pioneer*
ar ôl	*after*
arolygwr	*supervisor*
arolygydd	*supervisor*
arweinydd	*leader*
arwydd	*sign*
arwylfaen	*funerary stone*
asiedydd	*joiner*
aswy	*left (side)*
atgofion	*memories*
atgyweirio	*to repair*
atgyweiriwyd	*was repaired*
athrawes	*teacher (f)*
athro	*teacher (m)*
Awst	*August*
baban	*baby*
babandod	*infancy*
babanod	*babies*
bach	*little*
bachgen	*boy*
bardd	*poet*
Barnwyr, Barn.	*Judges*
bechgyn	*boys*
bedd	*grave*
beddfaen	*gravestone*
bedd-lech	*gravestone*
beddrod	*grave*
Bedyddwyr	*Baptists*
blaenor	*deacon*
blin	*grievous*
blodau	*flowers*
blodau ei ddyddiau	*prime of life*
blwydd, bl.	*year*
blwyddyn, bl.	*year*
blynedd, bl.	*year*

blynyddoedd	*years*
bod	*to be*
boddasant	*drowned (pl)*
boddi	*to drown*
boddodd	*drowned (sg)*
boddwyd	*was drowned*
Y Bont-faen	*Cowbridge*
bore	*morning*
brawd	*brother*
Brenhinoedd, Bren.	*Kings*
brodyr	*brothers*
brwydr	*battle*
Brycheiniog	*Breconshire*
Brynbuga	*Usk*
Bryste	*Bristol*
bu	*was*
buchedd	*life*
bu farw	*died (sg)*
bu foddi	*drowned (sg)*
bugail	*shepherd, minister of religion*
buont feirw	*died (pl)*
byd	*world*
bydwraig	*midwife*
byr	*short*
byth	*ever, never*
bywyd	*life*
cadben	*captain*
cael	*to get, to have, to receive*
Caer	*Chester*
Caerdydd	*Cardiff*
Caerfyrddin	*Carmarthen, Carmarthenshire*
Caergaint	*Canterbury*
Caergrawnt	*Cambridge*
Caergybi	*Holyhead*
Caernarfon	*Caernarvon, Caernarvonshire*
cafodd	*got, had, received (sg)*
cafodd ei eni	*was born (m)*
cafodd ei geni	*was born (f)*
cafodd ei ladd	*was killed (m)*
cafodd ei lladd	*was killed (f)*
Calan	*New Year's Day*
Calfinaidd	*Calvinistic*
cân	*song*
caniatad	*permission*
canlyn	*to follow, follows*
cant	*hundred*
canu	*to sing, singing*
capel	*chapel*
caredig	*loving, kind*
cariadus	*loving*
cariwr	*carrier*
carreg	*stone*
cartref	*home*
Casblaidd	*Wolf's Castle*
Casfuwch	*Castlebythe*
Casgwent	*Chepstow*
Casmael	*Puncheston*
Casnewydd	*Newport (Mon.)*
Casnewydd Bach	*Little Newcastle*
Castell Henri	*Henry's Moat*
Castell Nedd	*Neath*
Castellnewydd Emlyn	*Newcastle Emlyn*
cawsant	*got, had (pl)*
cefnder	*cousin (m)*
cenhadwr	*missionary*
cerddor	*musician*
cerfio	*to carve*
cerfiwyd	*was carved*
chwaer	*sister*
chwarel	*quarry*
chwarelwr	*quarryman*
chwech, chwe	*six*
chweched	*sixth*
chweched ar hugain	*twenty-sixth*
Chwefror	*February*
chwiorydd	*sisters*
chwith	*left (side)*
claddedigaeth	*funeral*
claddfa	*burial place, cemetery*

claddu	*to bury*
claddwyd	*was buried*
clerc	*clerk*
clochydd	*sexton*
clwyf	*wound*
clwyfau	*wounds*
clwyfo	*to wound*
clwyfwyd	*was wounded*
codi	*to raise*
codwr canu	*leader of singing*
codwyd	*was raised*
cof	*memory*
cofadail	*memorial*
cofeb	*memorial*
coffa	*memory*
coffadwriaeth	*memory*
coffhad	*memory*
cofgolofn	*memorial column*
cofiant	*memory*
cofio	*to remember*
cofion	*memories*
coleg	*college*
collasant	*lost (pl)*
colli	*to lose*
collodd	*lost (sg.)*
collwyd	*was lost*
colofn	*column*
corff, corph	*body*
corfflosgiad	*cremation*
Corinthiaid	*Corinthians*
crefftwr	*craftsman*
Crist	*Christ*
Cronicl, Cron.	*Chronicles*
crwynwr	*tanner*
crybwyll	*to mention*
crybwyllwyd	*was mentioned*
crydd	*shoemaker*
Crynwyr	*Quakers*
cu	*beloved*
curad	*curate*
cwympo	*to fall*
cwympodd	*fell (sg)*
cydweithiwr	*fellow worker*
cydweithwyr	*fellow workers*
cyfaill	*friend*
cyfarfod â	*to meet with*
cyfarfu â	*met with (sg)*
cyfarfyddodd â	*met with (sg)*
cyfarwyddwr addysg	*director of education*
cyfeillion	*friends*
cyfnither	*cousin (f)*
cyfnod	*period*
cyfodi	*to raise*
cyfodwyd	*was raised*
cyfreithiwr	*lawyer*
cyfrifol	*responsible*
cyhoeddus	*public*
cymdeithas	*society*
Cymdeithas y Cyfeillion	*Society of Friends*
cymdoges	*neighbour (f)*
cymeradwy	*worthy*
cymerodd	*took (sg)*
cymerwyd	*was taken*
cymryd	*to take*
cymwynaswr	*benefactor*
cymwys	*worthy*
cymydog	*neighbour (m)*
cyn	*before*
cyn-	*former*
cynghorydd	*councillor*
cyngor	*council*
cynhebrwng	*funeral*
cyntaf	*first*
cyrff, cyrph	*bodies*
cyrraedd	*to reach, reaching*
cysegr	*sanctuary*
cysegredig	*sacred*
cysga	*sleeps*
cysgu	*to sleep*
cystudd	*illness*
da	*good*
dadorchuddio	*to unveil*
dadorchuddiwyd	*was unveiled*
daearol	*earthly*
daearwyd	*was buried*
damwain	*accident*

damweiniol	*accidental*
darlithydd	*lecturer*
Datguddiad, Dat.	*Revelation*
dau	*two (m)*
de	*right (side), south*
defnyddiol	*useful*
deg	*ten*
degfed	*tenth*
degfed ar hugain	*thirtieth*
deheuol	*southern*
deng	*ten*
deilad	*tenant*
deintydd	*dentist*
deuddeg	*twelve*
deuddegfed	*twelfth*
deugain	*forty*
deunaw	*eighteen*
deunawfed	*eighteenth*
diacon	*deacon*
Diarhebion, Diar.	*Proverbs*
diflanedig	*transient*
dilledydd	*draper*
dilyn	*to follow*
dilynodd	*followed (sg)*
dinas	*city*
Dinbych	*Denbigh*
Dinbych-y-pysgod	*Tenby*
dirwestwr	*abstainer from alcohol*
disyfyd	*sudden*
disymwth	*sudden*
diwedd	*end*
diweddar	*late (has died), former*
diweddar o	*formerly from*
diwrnod	*day*
diwyd	*diligent*
diwygiwr	*revivalist*
dodi	*to put, to lay*
dodwyd	*was laid*
doeth	*wise*
Y Drenewydd	*Newtown*
dros, tros	*over*
drwy, trwy	*through*
drylliad	*wreck*
Duw	*God*
dwy	*two (f)*
dwyrain	*east*
dwyreiniol	*eastern*
dwys	*grave, serious*
dydd	*day*
dyddiau	*days*
Dydd Calan	*New Year's Day*
Dydd Gwener	*Friday*
Dydd Iau	*Thursday*
Dydd Llun	*Monday*
Dydd Mawrth	*Tuesday*
Dydd Mercher	*Wednesday*
Dydd Sadwrn	*Saturday*
Dydd Sul	*Sunday*
dyma	*here is*
dywededig	*said*
Ebrill	*April*
edmygwyr	*admirers*
yr Eidal	*Italy*
efengyl	*gospel*
eglwys	*church*
ei	*his, her*
ein	*our*
elusendy	*almshouse*
emyn	*hymn*
emynydd	*hymn writer*
englyn	*type of traditional poem*
enw	*name*
enwedig	*named*
enwi	*to name*
enwir	*is named*
enwyd	*was named*
er	*in (in memory of)*
eraill	*other (pl)*
erw	*acre*
Eseia	*Isaiah*
eto, etto	*also*
eu	*their*
ewythr	*uncle*

fel	*as, like*
Y Felinheli	*Port Dinorwic*
Y Fenai	*Menai Strait*
Y Fenni	*Abergavenny*
ficer	*vicar*
ffarmwr	*farmer*
fferyllydd	*pharmacist*
ffos	*ditch, trench*
ffosydd	*trenches*
y Fflint	*Flint, Flintshire*
Ffrainc	*France*
ffrind	*friend*
ffrwydriad	*explosion*
ffyddlon	*faithful*
fy	*my*
gair	*word*
geiriau	*words*
galw	*to call*
galwyd	*was called*
gan	*by*
ganed	*was born*
ganwyd	*was born*
garddwr	*gardener*
Y Garn	*Roch*
gefell	*twin*
gefeilliaid	*twins*
geiriadurwr	*writer of dictionaries*
gelyn	*enemy*
genedigaeth	*birth*
genedigol	*by birth*
geneth	*girl, daughter*
genethod	*girls, daughters*
geni	*to be born, birth*
ger	*near*
gerllaw	*near*
glanhau	*to clean*
glo	*coal*
glofa	*coalmine*
glöwr	*coal miner*
gobaith	*hope*
gof	*smith*
gofalu am	*to care for*
gofalus	*caring*
gogledd	*north*
gogleddol	*northern*
golygydd	*editor*
gorffen, gorphen	*to finish*
Gorffennaf, Gorphenhaf	*July*
gorffennodd, gorphenodd	*finished*
gorffwys, gorphwys	*to rest, rests*
gorffwysfa, gorphwysfa	*resting place*
gorffwyso, gorphwyso	*rests (sg), resting*
gorffwysodd, gorphwysodd	*rested (sg)*
goris	*beneath*
gorllewin	*west*
gorllewinol	*western*
gorsaf-feistr	*station master*
goruchwyliwr	*overseer*
gorwedd	*to lie, lies*
gorweddfa	*resting place*
gorweddle	*resting place*
gor-ŵyr	*great-grandson*
gor-wyres	*great-granddaughter*
gor-wyrion	*great-grandchildren*
gosod	*to put*
gosodwyd	*was put*
gwaith	*work*
Gwaredwr	*Redeemer*
gwas	*servant*
gwasanaethu	*to serve*
gweddillion	*remains*
gweddw	*widow*
gwehydd	*weaver*
gweinidog	*minister*
gweinidogaethu	*to minister, ministering*
gweithgar	*hardworking*
gweithiwr	*worker*
gwell	*better*
Gwener y Groglith	*Good Friday*
gwerthfawr	*valuable*

gwinllan	*vineyard*
gwirfoddolwr	*volunteer*
gwladgarwr	*patriot*
gwniadwraig	*dressmaker*
gwobr	*reward*
gŵr	*husband*
gwraig	*wife*
gwyddfa	*burial place*
gynt	*formerly*
gyrfa	*career, life*
hanner	*half*
hanner cant	*fifty*
hapus	*happy*
hawddgar	*beloved*
Hebreaid, Heb.	*Hebrews*
hedd	*peace*
heddgeidwad	*policeman*
heddlu	*police force*
heddwch	*peace*
hefyd	*also*
helbulus	*troubled*
hen	*old*
hen dadcu	*great-grandfather*
hen daid	*great-grandfather*
hen famgu	*great-grandmother*
hen nain	*great-grandmother*
henadur	*alderman*
henaint	*old age*
Hendy Gwyn ar Daf	*Whitland*
hir	*long*
hiraethus	*full of longing*
hoff	*beloved, favourite*
hoffus	*beloved*
hon	*this (f)*
huna	*sleeps*
hunfan	*sleeping place*
huno	*to sleep, sleeping*
hunodd	*fell asleep (sg)*
hunasant	*fell asleep (pl)*
Hwlffordd	*Haverfordwest*
hwn	*this (m)*
Hydref	*October*
hyfryd	*lovely*
hyn	*that, these*
hynaf	*oldest*
hynafieithydd	*antiquarian*
hynaws	*kind, loving*
i	*for, to*
'i	*his, her*
Iago, Iag.	*James*
iddi	*to her*
iddo	*to him*
iddynt	*to them*
yr Iesu	*Jesus*
Iesu Grist	*Jesus Christ*
ieuanc	*young*
ieuengaf	*youngest*
ifanc	*young*
ifancaf	*youngest*
Ioan	*John*
Ionawr	*January*
isod	*beneath*
Iwerddon	*Ireland*
Iwerydd	*Atlantic*
Lerpwl	*Liverpool*
lladd	*to kill*
lladdwyd	*was killed*
llafur	*work, labour*
llafurus	*hardworking*
Llanbedr y Fro	*Peterston-super-Ely*
Llanbedr Pont Steffan	*Lampeter*
Llanddunwyd	*Welsh St Donats*
Llandudoch	*St Dogmaels*
Llandudwg	*Tythegston*
Llanelwy	*St Asaph*
Llanfair ym Muallt	*Builth Wells*
Llanfihangel ar Elái	*Michaelston super Ely*
Llangrallo	*Coychurch*

Llanilltud Fawr	*Llantwit Major*
Llansanffraid (ar Elái)	*St Bride's super Ely*
llaw	*hand*
llawen	*joyful*
lle	*place, where*
llenor	*writer*
llestr	*vessel (= ship)*
Lloegr	*England*
llong	*ship*
llongddrylliad	*shipwreck*
llongwr	*sailor*
Llundain	*London*
llwch	*ashes*
llyfrwerthwr	*bookseller*
llyma	*here is*
Llynlleifiad	*Liverpool*
llys	*step (step son etc)*
llywydd	*captain (of a ship), president*
Luc	*Luke*
mab	*son*
maban	*baby*
mabandod	*infancy*
mabanod	*babies*
mabwysiedig	*adopted*
mae	*is*
maen	*stone*
maer	*mayor*
maes	*field*
Maesyfed	*New Radnor*
maes y gad	*field of battle*
maeth	*foster*
Mai	*May*
mai	*that*
maith	*long*
mam	*mother*
mamgu	*grandmother*
man	*place*
Manceinion	*Manchester*
Marc	*Mark*
marw	*to die, dead (sg)*
marwol	*mortal*
masnachwr, masnachydd	*merchant*
Mathew	*Matthew*
mawr	*big, great*
Mawrth	*March*
meddyg	*doctor*
Medi	*September*
Mehefin	*June*
meibion	*sons*
Meirionnydd	*Meirionethshire*
meirw	*to die, dead (pl)*
melinydd	*miller*
melys	*sweet*
merch	*daughter*
merched	*daughters*
Methodistiaid	*Methodists*
metron	*matron*
mewn	*in*
milfeddyg	*vet, farrier*
milwr	*soldier*
milwrol	*military*
mis	*month*
modd	*way*
modryb	*aunt*
Môn	*Anglesey*
môr	*sea*
Môr y Canoldir	*Mediterranean*
Môr Iwerydd	*Atlantic*
Y Môr Tawel	*Pacific*
mordaith	*voyage*
Morgannwg	*Glamorganshire*
morwr	*sailor*
mwynwr	*miner*
myfyriwr	*student*
mynwent	*churchyard, cemetery burial ground,*
Mynwy	*Monmouthshire*
'n	*in*
Nadolig	*Christmas*
nai	*nephew*
nain	*grandmother*
Nanhyfer, Nyfer	*Nevern*
naw	*nine*
nawfed	*ninth*

nawfed ar hugain	*twenty-ninth*
ni	*not*
nid	*not*
nith	*niece*
noda	*records (sg)*
nodi	*to record*
nychdod	*lingering illness*
Nyfer	*Nevern*
nyrs	*nurse*
o	*from, of*
odditanodd	*beneath*
oddiwrth	*from*
oed	*age*
oedd	*was*
oedran	*age*
offeiriad	*priest*
olaf	*last*
Palesteina	*Palestine*
parch	*respect*
Parchedig, Parch.	*Reverend, Rev.*
parchus	*respectful, respected*
Pasg	*Easter*
pedair	*four (f)*
pedwar	*four (m)*
pedwar ugain	*eighty*
pedwerydd	*fourth*
pedwerydd ar bymtheg	*nineteenth*
pedwerydd ar ddeg	*fourteenth*
pedwerydd ar hugain	*twenty-fourth*
peilot	*pilot (of a ship)*
peiriannydd	*engineer*
Penfro	*Pembroke, Pembrokeshire*
pennill	*verse of a poem*
pentref	*village*
Pen y bont ar Ogwr	*Bridgend*
perffaith	*perfect*
periglor	*priest*

perthnasau	*relatives*
Philipiaid, Phil.	*Philippians*
physigwr	*physician*
plant	*children*
plastrwr	*plasterer*
plentyn	*child*
plwyf, plwy	*parish*
Porthaethwy	*Menai Bridge*
prebendwr	*prebendary*
pregethu	*to preach, preaching*
pregethwr	*preacher*
Pregethwr, Preg.	*Ecclesiastes*
Presbyteriaid	*Presbyterians*
presennol	*present*
prif	*chief*
prifathrawes	*headmistress*
prifathro	*headmaster*
prifysgol	*university*
priod	*spouse (husband or wife)*
pryd	*time*
Prynwr	*Redeemer*
pumed	*fifth*
pumed ar hugain	*twenty-fifth*
pump, pum	*five*
pwll glo	*coalmine*
pymtheg	*fifteen*
pymthegfed	*fifteenth*
pythefnos	*fortnight*
'r	*the*
rhagddywededig	*aforesaid*
rhagflaenodd	*preceded*
rhagflaenu	*to precede*
Rhagfyr	*December*
rhag-grybwylledig	*above-named*
rhai	*those*
rhan	*part*
rheilffordd	*railway*
rheithor	*rector*
rhiant	*parent*
rhieni	*parents*
rhinweddol	*virtuous*
rhodd	*gift, donation*

rhoddi	*to lay, to give*
rhoddion	*gifts, donations*
rhoddodd	*laid, gave (sg)*
rhoddwyd	*was laid, was given*
rhoi	*to lay, to give*
Rhufeiniaid	*Romans*
rhwng	*between*
Rhydychen	*Oxford*
rhyfel	*war*
Saboth	*Sabbath*
saer	*carpenter*
saer coed	*carpenter*
saer llongau	*shipwright*
saer maen	*mason*
saith	*seven*
Salmau, Salm.	*Psalms*
salwch	*illness*
sant	*saint*
Sechareia, Sech.	*Zechariah*
sefydlydd	*founder*
sefydlwyr	*founders*
seithfed	*seventh*
seithfed ar hugain	*twenty-seventh*
Sephaneia, Seph.	*Zephaniah*
serch	*love*
serchog	*loving*
serchus	*loving*
siop	*shop*
sir	*county*
Sir Aberteifi	*Cardiganshire*
Sir Benfro	*Pembrokeshire*
Sir Ddinbych	*Denbighshire*
Sir Drefaldwyn	*Montgomeryshire*
Sir Faesyfed	*Radnorshire*
Sir Feirionnydd	*Meirionethshire*
Sir y Fflint	*Flintshire*
Sir Fôn	*Anglesey*
Sir Forgannwg	*Glamorganshire*
Sir Frycheiniog	*Breconshire*
Sir Fynwy	*Monmouthshire*
Sir Gaerfyrddin	*Carmarthen-shire*
Sir Gaernarfon	*Caernarvon-shire*
sirydd	*sheriff*
storm	*storm*
suddiad	*sinking*
suddo	*to sink*
suddodd	*sank (sg)*
Sulgwyn	*Whit Sunday*
Sul y Pasg	*Easter Sunday*
swydd	*county*
swydd	*job, post*
swyddog	*officer*
sydd	*is*
sydyn	*sudden*
sylfaenwyr	*founders*
sylfaenydd	*founder*
symud	*to move*
symudwyd	*was moved*
syrthio	*to fall*
syrthiodd	*fell (sg)*
Tachwedd	*November*
tad	*father*
tadcu	*grandfather*
taid	*grandfather*
tair	*three (f)*
Talacharn (Lacharn)	*Laugharne*
talu	*to pay*
talwyd	*was paid*
tanchwa	*explosion*
tangnefedd	*peace*
tanysgrifiadau	*subscriptions*
tawel	*quiet*
teg	*fair*
telynor	*harpist (m)*
telynores	*harpist (f)*
terfysglyd	*troubled*
teulu	*family*
teyrnged	*tribute*
Thesaloniaid, Thes.	*Thessalonians*
Timotheus, Tim.	*Timothy*
tloty	*poorhouse*
trallodus	*sorrowful*
Y Trallwm, Y Trallwng	*Welshpool*
Treamlod	*Ambleston*

Trebefered	*Boverton*
tref, tre	*town*
Trefaldwyn	*Montgomery, Montgomeryshire*
Trefdraeth	*Newport (Pembs)*
treflan	*small town*
Trefflemin	*Flemingston*
Trefnyddion	*Methodists*
Treforus	*Morriston*
Trefyclo	*Knighton*
Treletert	*Letterston*
Tremarchog	*St Nicholas*
Tresimwn	*Bonvilston*
treuliau	*costs*
Trewyddel	*Moylegrove*
tri	*three (m)*
trigain	*sixty*
tros, dros	*over*
trwy, drwy	*through*
trwm	*heavy*
trydydd	*third*
trydydd ar ddeg	*thirteenth*
trydydd ar hugain	*twenty-third*
trysorydd	*treasurer*
tŷ	*house*
tŷ cwrdd	*chapel, meeting house*
Tyddewi	*St David's*
tyner	*tender*
'u	*their*
uchod	*above*
ugain	*twenty*
ugeinfed	*twentieth*
un	*one*
un ar ddeg	*eleven*
undeb	*union*
Undodwyr	*Unitarians*
unfed ar bymtheg	*sixteenth*
unfed ar ddeg	*eleventh*
unfed ar ddeg ar hugain	*thirty-first*
unfed ar hugain	*twenty-first*
unig	*only*
uwch	*above*
warden	*churchwarden*
Y Waun	*Chirk*
wedi	*after*
wele	*behold*
Wesleyaid	*Wesleyans*
Wesleyaidd	*Wesleyan*
yr Wyddgrug	*Mold*
ŵyr	*grandson*
wyres	*grand-daughter*
wyresau	*grand-daughters*
wyrion	*grandchildren*
wyth	*eight*
wythfed	*eighth*
wythfed ar hugain	*twenty-eighth*
wythnos	*week*
y	*the*
ym	*in*
yma	*here, this*
ymadael â	*to depart from*
ymadawodd â	*departed from (sg.)*
ymadawsant â	*departed from (pl.)*
ymdrechgar	*hard working*
ymgeledd	*support*
ymroddedig	*devoted*
yn	*in*
Ynad Heddwch, YH	*Justice of the peace, JP*
yng	*in*
ynghanol	*in the midst of*
ynghyd	*together*
yng nghyfraith	*in law, step*
yno	*there*
Ynys Enlli	*Bardsey*
yr	*the*
y rhai a	*who (pl)*
yr hon a	*who (f)*
yr hwn a	*who (m)*
yr un	*the same*
ysbaid	*period*
ysbyty, ysbytty	*hospital*

ysgol	*school*
ysgol Sabothol	*Sunday School*
ysgol Sul	*Sunday School*
ysgolfeistr	*schoolmaster*
ysgolfeistres	*school mistress*
ysgrifennydd	*secretary*
ystlys	*side*
yw	*is*

16

Further reading

This is a practical handbook, intended to help you deal with a very specific kind of material, the Welsh language inscriptions on gravestones. It is quite possible, however, that you may want to follow up some aspects of this work in a little more depth, and the suggestions which follow should provide some useful extra background information.

Dictionaries

If the inscription you are reading includes unusual phrases, which are not in the word list at the end of this book, then you may need to consult a Welsh-English dictionary. There are many of these, but you may find the following useful.

> Heini Gruffudd, *The Welsh Learner's Dictionary* (Y Lolfa, 2002) – this is useful in that it tells you when you might need to look for a word under a different initial letter because of a mutation.

> Gareth King, *The Pocket Modern Welsh Dictionary* (Oxford University Press, 2000)

Learning Welsh

You may now feel that it is worth making the effort and learning some Welsh, so that you can research your Welsh-speaking ancestors more effectively. Either of these will give you a good basic grounding in the language.

> Phyl Brake, *Welsh in Three Months* (Dorling Kindersley, 1998)

Julie Brake and Christine Jones, *Teach Yourself Welsh* (Hodder and Stoughton, 2003)

If you would like to attend a Welsh course and learn alongside other people, ring Learn Direct on 0800 101 901, or email info@welshforadults.org to find out when and where they are held in your area. If you live outside Wales, or would find it difficult to attend a class, then another possibility is to learn on-line. Introductory distance-learning Welsh courses are run by the University of Wales Trinity Saint David and by the Open University.

Personal names

These two books explain the background to the development of surnames in Wales. What do these names mean? What kind of variants have developed? In which parts of Wales are they are most commonly found?

Thomas John and Prys Morgan, *Welsh Surnames* (University of Wales Press, 1985)

John and Sheila Rowlands, *The Surnames of Wales* (Federation of Family History Societies (Publications) Ltd, 1996)

Place-names

If you come across unfamiliar Welsh place-names, it is worth checking in any of these books to see if there is a corresponding English name. The second and third will also explain the meaning of some of the place-names involved.

Elwyn Davies (ed.) *A Gazetteer of Welsh Place-names* (University of Wales Press, 1967)

Hywel Wyn Owen and Richard Morgan, *Dictionary of the Place-Names of Wales* (Gomer Press, 2007)

Anthony Lias, *Place-name Detective* (Gwasg Carreg Gwalch, 2008)

History of the Welsh language

Many people find that their family was originally Welsh-speaking, but lost the language at some point and now speak only English. This gradual loss of the language has been an important feature of the history of Wales, and if you are interested in seeing how this happened and what the forces involved were, this short introduction will fill in some of the background.

Janet Davies, *The Welsh Language: A Pocket Guide* (University of Wales Press and Western Mail, 1999)

Family history

If you are new to family history in Wales, and are finding the whole process rather confusing, then the following introduction may prove useful.

John Rowlands and others (eds.), *Welsh Family History: a Guide to Research* (Association of Family History Societies of Wales, 1993)

National Library of Wales, Aberystwyth

The National Library holds many records from Wales, including births, marriages and deaths, census returns, parish registers, diocesan records, etc. The staff are always helpful. The Library is open Monday to Friday, 9.30 am – 6.00 pm. and with a restricted service on Saturdays. Access is by reader's ticket. There is a shop and café. For more information telephone 01970 632933, or see the website: www.llgc.org.uk.

If you have been working on your own, and would like to contact other people who are interested in family history, try contacting the **Association of Family History Societies of Wales**. This overall group includes the following local Family History Societies – Cardiganshire, Clwyd, Dyfed, Glamorgan, Gwent, Gwynedd, Montgomeryshire and Powys. Go to the web address below, which will allow you to click through to the local Family History Society relevant to your own interests: www.fhswales.org.uk.

The **Family History Societies** publish transcripts, as paper copies or on microfiche, of the memorial inscriptions found in some, though not all, of the churchyards, burial grounds and cemeteries in their area. If you are fairly sure that you know where your family graves are, but are unable go there yourself, then it may be worth finding out if there is a transcript and having a look at it as a first step.

Further enjoyable reading on Industrial Heritage

Visit our website for further information:

www.carreg-gwalch.com

Orders can be placed on our

On-line Shop